01 Games
for Social Skills

Jenny Mosley

d Helen Sonnet

Acknowledgements

Having fun is one of the best ways to learn. If you feel happy, then you are positive, more able to relate to others and more open to taking learning risks. I should like to thank all the long-term groups I teach for helping to make our sessions fun. My own fund of games keeps growing and my team of consultants certainly also carry around a magic bag of first-class games. It is owing to working with children and adults over the years that Helen and I have been able to research the potential of games to help the development of children's personal and social skills.

In particular, I should like to thank Grace Scott, Primary Advisor for East Ayrshire – not only for her endless enthusiasm but also, recently, for the merry band of teachers who attended one of my accredited Train the Trainers groups. We spent some time in groups looking at the importance and relevance of games to social skills and that certainly helped to hone my own ideas. Helen, too, with her own four children and her work in a local primary school, is brilliant at devising new games and understanding exactly how a game helps to move certain children forward in their skills and development. I should also like to thank Corin Redsell for his endless patient editing and for being a very calm voice in contrast to my, oft times, strident high-pitched one. I am grateful to Sue Cooper for her valuable social skills that enabled LDA and our own team to work together easily and harmoniously.

Jenny Mosley

101 Games for Social Skills

MT00553

© Jenny Mosley and Helen Sonnet

Illustrations by Rebecca Barnes

ISBN-13: 978 1 85503 370 2

All rights reserved

First published 2003

Reprinted 2003 (twice), 2004 (twice), 2005 (twice), 2006, 2007, 2009, 2010 (twice), 2011, 2012, 2013 (twice), 2014

The rights of Jenny Mosley and Helen Sonnet to be identified as the authors of this work have been asserted by them in accordance with sections 77 and 78 of the Copyright, Designs and Patents Act 1988.

Printed in the UK for LDA

LDA, Victoria Business Park, Pintail Close, Netherfield, Nottingham, NG4 2SG

Contents

Thinking

Concentrating

Thinking of others

Working together

Enhancing communication skills

Skills for out and about

Celebrating together

Introduction

From the moment of birth every child begins a social journey. On this journey, children learn that different circumstances are governed by distinct rules and conventions of behaviour. We are all, as we grow up, required to become aware of what is, and what is not, expected of us in each of the settings we find ourselves in. Children quickly come to know that their personal happiness and self-esteem are intricately linked with their ability to interact appropriately and to form positive relationships in every demanding and complicated situation. They also grasp the fact that a great deal of skill is involved in the process of becoming 'socialised'.

> People who live without a shared set of values and rules cannot live as a people. The human condition is composed of social realities. (Hugh Brody)

The journey of life is not a simple one. Children must learn that being part of a community requires that they share, are less demanding and wait their turn – are 'cooperative'. The adults who are involved with children influence the way in which they enter society, shape aspects of their character and affect the rate at which this kind of development takes place. Teachers and schools have a vital role to play in this process because the influences on the child within the home are sometimes not harmonious with the values, interests and behavioural norms that they encounter outside it.

If children have learned to behave, think and communicate in ways that are different from, or opposed to, those they encounter in the wider world, they may become confused and find it difficult to adjust. They may discover that behaviours that are tolerated at home cause trouble in other situations. The assistance offered by schools may be crucial, making or breaking children's potential to mature into adults who can confidently take their place in the world knowing that they are able to work, communicate and relate effectively.

Children learn interpersonal skills by watching and copying others. One of the many benefits that the Quality Circle Time Model offers to teachers is the opportunity to model positive behaviour through the enjoyable and child-centred means of games and activities. The kinds of games presented in this book provide children with the chance to rehearse social skills in a non-threatening environment that offers support and constructive feedback.

Through role-play games children can experience what it will be like in environments and situations that they have not yet encountered. Children watch and learn from other children and adults when they model the appropriate behaviour for a particular situation. Games are not seen as work, so less successful children will not be defensive in their approach to them. Games capture the imagination, and they are entertaining, multi-sensory and active. Most important, children seem to have an innate interest in playing them. The games in this book are intrinsically sociable and, as such, make ideal vehicles for teaching the skills that children need to become socially aware and confident. The games will also help children to unravel and solve social problems and change learnt patterns of anti-social behaviour.

101 Games for Social Skills is divided into two parts. The first part includes games that teach the following abilities that help children to develop social skills: looking, listening, speaking, thinking and concentrating. The games provide the opportunity for individuals to think about these skills and to practise them in a group situation.

The second part of the book consolidates those five abilities and provides opportunities for children to apply them in appropriate social contexts. Each game has a specific learning outcome and is designed to reinforce interpersonal skills, focus on social observations or provide an opportunity to practise a particular skill.

The games can be incorporated into regular Circle Times or used as part of the curriculum for Personal, Social and Health Education and Citizenship. They can also be adapted to suit the specific needs of your particular class.

As you help children on their social journey, we hope that you will find these games both effective and enjoyable. Have fun!

Looking

The games in this section focus on the joint looking activities of seeing and watching. Children are encouraged to appreciate the difference between these two activities and also to discover how important looking is to learning.

The troublesome tray

This game encourages children to concentrate when they use their looking skills.

Resources

A tray, a tea towel and a selection of small objects. These could include a pencil, a pencil sharpener, a pair of scissors, an envelope, a safety pin, a rubber, a piece of chalk.

What to do

Lay out a number of the small objects on the tray. The number of objects should reflect the age and ability of the children involved. You might start with four objects for young children and between eight and twelve for older children. Allow the children a minute to study the objects, cover the tray with the tea towel and take away one of the objects, making sure that the children cannot see what it is. Remove the tea towel and show the tray to the children again. Ask a volunteer to say what they think is missing from the tray. If they guess correctly, they could secretly remove one object from the covered tray in the next round.

Comments

You will quickly get a feel for how easy or difficult the children are finding this game, and you can then increase or decrease the number of objects accordingly. Change the set of objects regularly so that the children do not become familiar with the items used.

A change of clothes

This is another simple game that promotes careful looking rather than just seeing.

Resources

A bag of dressing-up clothes

What to do

Ask a volunteer to put on several items from the bag of dressing-up clothes and to stand in the centre of the circle. Ask the other children to look very carefully at what that child is wearing. Then tell the children in the circle to turn round and close their eyes whilst the child who dressed up takes off one item of the dressing-up clothes they are wearing. Alternatively, the child could remove the item of clothing outside the room if an adult is available to supervise them. Once the child has returned to the centre of the circle, or the children in the circle have turned round and opened their eyes, invite the children to say what piece of clothing has been removed.

Comments

With older children, you can make the changes more subtle. Instead of removing an item of clothing, it could be worn in a slightly different way – such as wearing a scarf undone instead of tied in a knot, or changing one scarf for a different one. This is a game in which children could think up their own ways of making what happens more complex.

Thinking faces

In this game children use visual cues to draw on their
knowledge and experience of life.

Resources

Cut out a selection of illustrations of people from magazines. Try
to make them as varied as possible and not too small. You might
include such people as a clown, a toddler, an elderly person, a
ballerina, a soldier, a juggler, someone wearing flippers. Paste these
pictures onto card and cut them out.

What to do

Tell the children that you are going to show them a series of
pictures of people. Tell them that as they see each person they must
imagine that they are that person and then walk around the room
as they think that person would. Before trying the next illustration,
discuss with the children what they know about the previous
illustration and how that influenced the way in which they decided
to walk. You could then give them another opportunity to try the
game again.

Comments

With older children, you could introduce further activities by using
two or more of the pictures at a time. They could act out a
conversation or short scene involving those people. Ask the children
to think about how the people involved in the scene may react.
Discuss how we pick up a lot of clues about a person or a situation
from visual details.

Signal success

This is an energetic game in which children need to look and concentrate in order to follow the visual instructions which they are given.

Resources

Enlarged photocopied versions of signal cards (see page 130)

What to do

Show the signal cards to the children and explain to them what action each one represents. Go through the cards and let the children practise the relevant action for each of them. Tell the children that they are going to play a game in which you will hold up one of the cards and they must perform the relevant action until you hold up a different card. They must then change to the new action. Encourage the children to be vigilant and explain that you may change the card at any time.

Comments

Once the children are comfortable with the different signals, you can vary the pace at which you swap the cards. You can also say that the children who are slowest to respond will be out. Older children may enjoy thinking up their own sets of signals.

Ready for action

This is an enjoyable game that involves the children in both
looking carefully and concentrating.

Resources

None

What to do

Agree with the children a selection of actions that correspond to
visual cues given by the leader of the game. For example:

When the leader touches their elbow, the children jump on the
spot.
When the leader touches their ear, the children do bunny jumps.
When the leader wiggles their nose, the children sit on the
floor.
When the leader raises their arms, the children hop on the spot.
When the leader folds their arms, the children lie down.

Play a game in which the children must react correctly to the visual
cue you give. They must watch you carefully to see when you
perform the next cue so that they are ready to change the action.

Comments

Children will enjoy taking turns at giving the cues, once they are
familiar with this game. You could also ask children to come up with
some different visual cues.

Catch the fox's tail

This is a fast, active game that focuses on being alert
and observant.

Resources

Coloured bands of material. You need plenty of space to move
around in.

What to do

The children tuck the bands into their waistbands at the back,
leaving enough material hanging to represent a fox's tail. When you
say 'Go', the children run around trying to capture the tails of the
other foxes, at the same time keeping their own tails intact. If their
tail is taken, the child sits on the side of the playing area until the
end of the game. They keep any tails that they captured before they
lost their own. Players are allowed to touch only the tail of another
fox; no other bodily contact is permitted. Allow a couple of minutes
for this game, then call the group together to see who has collected
the most tails and who has managed to keep theirs. Redistribute
the captured tails and play the game again.

Comments

Once the children are familiar with this game, you will have to
check that they leave enough of the band showing to represent
their tail. They very quickly learn that the shorter the tail, the more
difficult it is to grab.

What am I doing?

In this game the children have to think about how to
make their actions clear and concise so that they provide the
correct visual clues for the other children to guess
what they are doing.

Resources

A list of mimes (see page 131)

What to do

Give a child a mime from the list to perform. The other children can take turns to guess what the child is miming. The child who guesses correctly can perform the next mime if they wish.

The children could work in two teams, each team having a list of mimes. Children in each team take it in turn to perform the next mime on their list.

Comments

Ask the children to think up their own ideas for mimes that can be added to the list. You could also divide the class into groups of 5 or 6 and ask them to work out a mime between them. They could focus on an event such as a birthday party or visit to the circus.

Traffic chant

This energetic game helps children to observe others carefully.

Resources

None. Plenty of space to play in is needed.

What to do

Teach the children the following chant.

> *Boats and planes*
> *Cars and trains*
> *Boats and planes and cars and trains*
> *Travel round the world.*

Next, teach the children the actions relating to the chant.

> *Boat* – pretend to be paddling a canoe.
> *Plane* – arms held out like wings.
> *Car* – pretend to be holding a steering wheel.
> *Train* – arms rotating by your side like pistons.
> *World* – turn around on the spot.

When they have performed the song a few times and are fairly confident, speed up the words. See how fast they can do this before most of them fail to keep up with the actions.

As a variation, chant the song but leave out a mode of transport each time. The children must still perform the relevant action.

Comments

Let the children choose their own actions to go with a nursery rhyme or pop song.

Pass it along

This game has two elements – the first focuses on careful looking and the second on acting skills.

Resources

A small object such as a ball

What to do

The children stand in a circle, facing inwards. One child is chosen to stand in the middle of the circle. The other children pass the ball round the circle behind their backs. The child in the centre has to guess where the ball is. When they think they know where the ball is, they say 'Stop'. All the children then stand still while the child makes two guesses of where the ball is. If their guess is correct, they swap places with the child who had the ball. If the child in the centre guesses incorrectly, the game resumes. The player in the centre may have up to three turns.

To make the task more challenging, the child in the centre could close their eyes whilst the ball is passed round the circle and the children in the circle count down from 5 to 0. When they get to 0 the child in the centre opens their eyes and the game continues as above. In addition, some children could pretend to pass the ball round the circle to confuse the child in the centre.

Comments

You can add another element of difficulty to the game by using two objects passed in opposite directions round the circle. The child in the centre has to try to spot both objects when they call 'Stop'.

Back writing

The children have to use their visual perception in addition to normal vision in this team game.

Resources

Paper, two pencils, shape cards (see page 132)

What to do

Divide the group into two teams. Ask the children in each team to line up, one behind the other. Give the child at the front of each team a piece of paper and a pencil, and the child at the back a shape card. Tell the child at the back to draw this shape, using their index finger, on the back of the child in front of them. The child in front concentrates on the shape being drawn on their back, then, without looking at the card, attempts to draw the shape on the back of the child in front of them and so on up the line. When the drawing reaches the beginning of the line, the child at the front draws the shape on their piece of paper. The team that draws the shape closest to the original wins a point for their team. The child at the front then moves to the back of the line and the game continues with a new shape card.

Comments

Encourage the children to draw slowly and carefully on the next child's back so that they make a clear impression of the shape. You can start with simple shapes and make them more complex as the children become more proficient.

Further activities

Watch this space

This activity can be done over a period of several days. Put the children into pairs and ask them to watch a scene from a video for 1 minute. They must write down everything they can see. They then watch the scene again and see how many details they noticed. After this they could devise some questions for another group of children to answer after they have watched the same scene.

Photo-fit

Collect pictures of people from magazines – these need not be people whom the children will recognise. Put the children into pairs and give each child a picture to study. After a minute tell them to swap photographs with their partner. In turn they ask their partner questions about the person they originally had. They get a point for each correct answer.

Look what's new

Use a whiteboard or a large sheet of card. Draw a picture. Each time the children go out of the room, change or add one thing to the picture. See how many of the children can spot the changes.

Spot the difference

Make or copy enough pages of a spot-the-difference drawing for each child. Have a race to see who can find all the differences first.

A different action

Work out a routine of actions with the children. Each time you perform the routine, change one action. See who notices what has been changed.

Listening

The games in this section focus on helping the children to listen attentively in order to participate successfully in the activities. Also, children are encouraged to concentrate on one source of sound and filter out extraneous noises.

Who's talking now?

Children always enjoy a guessing game and this one can provide lots of fun over mistaken identities.

Resources

A blindfold

What to do

A child is chosen to be the monarch and to stand in the centre of the circle, wearing the blindfold. On the command of 'Go' the other children walk around the circle until the monarch calls 'Stop'. The monarch then points in front of them and asks 'Who goes there? Friend or foe?' The child who is being pointed at answers 'Why, friend, of course, Your Majesty.' The monarch tries to guess the identity of the speaker. If they guess correctly, the monarch and child swap places. If the guess is incorrect, the monarch stays in the centre and a new game begins. A child can be a monarch for up to three games.

Comments

It is probably a good idea to practise what the children have to say before you begin the game. Tell them they must answer in their real voices. However, if you find that the children are guessing correctly a lot of the time, they can try to disguise their voices when they answer, adding a further element of fun.

Chain reaction

This game requires the children to stay alert and ready to respond. It can be great fun when played at a really fast pace.

Resources

None

What to do

The children stand in a circle. The object of the game is to end with all the children sitting down. A child (A) is chosen to begin the game. They call out the name of another child (B) across the circle. Child A then sits down. Child B calls the name of a third child (C), then child B sits down. Child C calls the name of a fourth child (D) and so on. If any child hesitates or does not respond to being called, all the children must stand up and the game begins again with a different child starting it.

Comments

The real fun of the game is to see how fast it can be completed. You could use a timer and establish a class record, which children could then try to break.

Let me tell you a story

The children have to listen carefully for the cue words in the story and react accordingly.

Resources

Story with cue words (see page 133)

What to do

The children should sit on chairs in a circle. Explain to them that you are going to read them a story that contains certain cue words. Each time you say a cue word they must perform a specific action. Let them practise the different actions for the cue words. Tell the children that if they perform the wrong action or are the slowest to respond, they will be out. Then read the story, judging after each cue word who is out. At the end see how many children are left and commend them for listening so well on that occasion.

Comments

If you are concerned about children being 'out', just read through the story and let all the children play until the end. You can commend those particular children whom you saw responding quickly and correctly.

Who has the ball?

This game helps children to focus on one particular sound,
filtering out other noises that are unimportant.

Resources

A small ball and a blindfold

What to do

The children stand in a circle, facing inwards. A child is chosen to
stand in the centre of the circle, wearing the blindfold. The children
pass the ball around the circle until the child in the centre calls
'Stop'. The child then asks the question 'Who has got the ball?' The
child with the ball responds 'I have got the ball.' At the same time,
all the other children say 'My name is . . .' The child in the centre
has to listen carefully and point in the direction of the speaker with
the ball. If the direction is correct, the two children swap places. If
not, the child can ask up to three times before they swap with
another child.

Comments

The ball must be passed quietly around the circle, as undue noise
will give away its location. Warn the children not to be loud in their
responses, otherwise the child in the centre will be overwhelmed by
the noise.

Who was the trickster?

This is an enjoyable circle game to keep the children alert and listening for their names to be called out. They must also listen to each other so they are able to clap in time to the rhythm of the chant.

Resources

None

What to do

The children sit in a circle. They clap to the rhythm of the first two lines and continue to do this each time they are repeated. Use names of children in the circle.

Class: *Who was the trickster awake last night?*
Roaming the house 'til morning light?

Teacher: [Child A's name] was the trickster ready to strike.

Child A: Oh no, no, I shake my head,
I was tucked up asleep in bed.

Class: *Then who was the trickster awake last night?*
Roaming the house 'til morning light?

Child A: [Child B's name] was the trickster ready to strike.

Child B: Oh no, no, I shake my head
I was tucked up safe in bed.

Class: *Then who was the trickster etc.*

Comments

If you want to make sure that everyone has a turn, the children could begin the game standing, then sit down once they have had their go, continuing to join in with the chant. Once they know the chant well, a child could take the teacher's role.

Double trouble

In this game the children have to try to listen to one sound only, even though someone is deliberately trying to distract them.

Resources

Fact cards (see page 134 for fact cards for 8-year-old children)

What to do

Divide the children into groups of 4. Child A will be the listener, children B and C the speakers, and child D the adjudicator. The speakers are given two different fact cards, which they read through to themselves. Child D tells child A that they must listen to only one speaker; child A can decide which one. Both child B and child C stand facing child A, the same distance away. Child D counts 'One, two, three, go!' and both speakers read their cards aloud at the same time, in normal speaking voices. When they have finished, child D asks child A the questions on the card of the speaker whom they chose, followed by the questions on the card of the other speaker. Child D makes a note of the correct answers relating to both cards. The children change roles and collect a new pair of fact cards. They repeat the process until all four have had a turn at listening.

Comments

Find out how many children managed to get all three answers correct for the chosen speaker's card, and how many got answers correct for the second speaker's card. Discuss what made it difficult or easy to focus on one speaker and filter out what the other was saying.

Tongue twisters

In this game children have to think about the sound of
words. They must listen and concentrate.

Resources

Paper and pencils

What to do

Give the children a few examples of tongue twisters – for example
'She sells seashells on the seashore' and 'Peter Piper picked a peck
of pickled peppers.' Discuss with the children what makes tongue
twisters difficult to say. Arrange the children into pairs and give
each pair a piece of paper and a pencil. Ask the children to have a
go at writing their own tongue twisters. When they have finished,
they can swap their ideas with those of other pairs.

Comments

Have a competition to see who can say a tongue twister the fastest
without making any mistake.

Vary the volume

This game encourages the children to consider how noise affects our behaviour.

Resources

A tape/CD player. Space for the children to move around in.

What to do

Tell the children that you want them to move around in a manner suggested by the music. Put the music on at normal volume for 30 seconds, then turn it up very loud for 1 minute, followed by very quiet for 1 minute. Switch the music off and call the children back to you. Ask them how the volume affected their movements. Tell them that you are going to play the music again and that you will vary the volume. They must do small movements when the music is quiet and big movements when it is loud. If you change the volume gradually they must make the change in their movements gradual, but if you go from very quiet straight to very loud they must respond quickly.

Comments

Talk to the children about when music might be played at different volumes and why. For example, soft music might be played to help you relax at the dentist's or when you are trying to get to sleep. Loud and stirring music might be played to rouse emotions – for example pop music at a disco or brass-band music at a parade.

Racing whispers

In this game the children must listen carefully and speak clearly to be successful.

Resources

None. Enough space for the children to spread out.

What to do

Put the children into two teams and ask each team to stand in line, with a clear space between the children. This is so that only those who are at the front of the line hear the whispered message. Sit on a chair some distance away from the children. Explain to them that you will whisper an action to the two children at the front of each line. These children whisper the action to the second children in their line, who whisper it to the third and so on. When the whisper reaches the last child in the line, they run up to you and perform the action. You can give points for how accurate the action is. Then whisper a new command to this child, who goes to the front of their line and the process is repeated. Actions could include, for example, hop three times on the spot, bend down and touch your toes.

Comments

Warn the children that they can only whisper and only give the message once. This means they need to communicate slowly and clearly and listen carefully when they receive a message.

Clap this way

The children have to listen to the beat of the music and your instructions in this game, so they must concentrate and be alert.

Resources

A tape/CD player and a piece of music with a clearly defined beat to clap to

What to do

Ask the children to stand in a circle. Tell them that they are going to clap to the rhythm of a piece of music. At the same time you are also going to call out instructions that they must follow. The instructions could include:

> *Clap high* (clap above your head), *1, 2, 3, 4.*
> *Clap low* (clap down by your knees), *1, 2, 3, 4.*
> *Clap to the right, 1, 2, 3, 4.*
> *Clap to the left, 1, 2, 3, 4.*
> *Clap hands with your partner* (both hands together), *1, 2, 3, 4.*
> *Clap and turn around, 1, 2, 3, 4.*

Comments

Decide beforehand which way the children are going to turn when they clap hands with a partner; otherwise there will be chaos. Let the children establish the rhythmic clapping to the music before you call out the instructions.

Further activities

Twirl your partner

Find a barn-dance routine or make up some suitable movements to a piece of music that you can call out for the children to follow.

Funny adjectives

Look at how the BFG talks in the book by Roald Dahl. Ask the children if they like the adjectives he uses and why. Ask them to make up some words to describe worms; a really comfortable bed; a long, tiring journey; and how they feel when they fall over.

Sounds I really like

Ask the children to write down their ten favourite sounds – for example the jingle played by an ice-cream van, a bath running. Then ask them for their ten least favourite everyday sounds.

What happens next?

Read an interesting but incomplete sentence to the children and ask them to think what happens next – for example 'The door of the spacecraft slid silently open and . . .'

Story tape

Play a story tape to the children as a change from reading to them yourself. Establish a listening corner that the children can use to listen to story tapes using headphones.

Voices

Out of hearing of the group, record all the children saying a sentence. Play back the recording to see if the children can recognise who is talking.

Speaking

The games in this section encourage the children to talk within the group. The games begin with group speaking and progress to individuals talking.

The tone of my voice

This game is good fun. Shyer children are supported by the whole group speaking together.

Resources

None

What to do

Teach the children the following chant:

> *We're the children from . . . and we like to speak in this way. Hello,* [leader's name], *hello, children. We hope you have a nice day.*

The leader of the game then replies 'Say it again . . .' and asks a child to volunteer a way of speaking – for example happily, grumpily, fearfully, in an alien language, very quietly, with a bad cold. The group then repeat the chant in the manner suggested.

Comments

Brainstorm the possible ways of speaking before you begin playing, to give the children an idea of the sort of tones they could use.

Favourite things

In this game most of the speaking is again supported
by the whole group, giving the children the opportunity to
forget their shyness and join in the activity. Individual
talking is on a voluntary basis, so no-one feels
pressurised into having to speak.

Resources

None

What to do

Teach the children in the circle the following chant:

All of us have favourite things, that we really like.
A doll, a book, some rollerblades, a keepsake or a bike.
Class . . . is here together, every girl and boy.
We'll talk about our favourite things and what we all enjoy.

Invite the children to complete the sentence stem 'My favourite
thing is . . . '

Comments

With younger children it may be an idea to talk them through what
they might choose as their favourite thing. It need not be a toy or
anything big; it could be a photograph, a seashell from a holiday, or
the pond in their garden. Older children might like to add the
reason for choosing their favourite thing.

Who can think of something . . . ?

This game gives support to individuals, who participate by using the sentence stem provided. The children are asked to volunteer an answer but do have the opportunity to pass.

Resources

None

What to do

Ask a series of questions to which the children volunteer answers – for example:

Who can think of something heavy?
Something heavy is . . .

Choose one child to answer. Other questions could include: something furry, something loud, something scary, something big, something hard, something cold.

Comments

Older children might like to take turns to name the category.

Special delivery

This game involves both group and individual speaking.
Children can decide whether or not to speak.

Resources

None

What to do

Choose a child to be the delivery person. The other children sit in a circle. They say together:

> *Postman/lady, postman/lady, is there a pack,*
> *A letter or a parcel for me in your sack?*
> *Postman/lady, postman/lady, down our way,*
> *I hope that you call on me today.*

While the children are saying this, the delivery person walks around inside the circle. At the end of the verse all the children who would like the delivery person to call hold out their hands. The delivery person chooses three children to make deliveries to. These children decide what the delivery person has given them – for example a letter from a friend, a present, something they have ordered. Each child in turn describes to the others what the delivery person has brought them. A new delivery person is chosen and the game is repeated.

Comments

It might be a good idea to brainstorm all the things that could be delivered before the game, so that the children have a chance to think what they would wish the delivery person to bring to them.

Who can . . . ?

In this game the children speak together as a group, but can also volunteer to speak individually.

Resources

None

What to do

This game involves question-and-answer responses. Begin the game by asking the children a question such as:

> *Who in the group can hop?* (repeat)
> *Put your hand up, one, two, three.*
> *Who in the group can hop?*

The children put up their hands in response to the question. You choose one child, who either performs or mimes the action. That child can think of another action, which they then ask the group or can say along with the rest of the group. Actions could include: jumping, brushing teeth, riding a bicycle, swimming, playing football.

Comments

If the children are quite confident about speaking out in front of the group, you can play the game with individual children asking the questions and choosing who will answer. With younger children you can also repeat the verse when a child has performed an action, substituting the child's name for 'who' in the rhyme.

Greetings

This game encourages all the children in the group to respond to the greeting of their peers. The response is simple and formulaic so that children will not worry about what they are going to say.

Resources

None

What to do

Arrange the children in a circle so that some confident children who can start the action are next to each other. One child is chosen to be greeted first. The children then say the following together:

We are the children in our group, we'll welcome everyone.
We'd like to say hello to . . .

The first child who has been greeted responds by saying 'Hello, everyone.' Play then moves to the child on the left of the child who has just been greeted.

Comments

One way of removing any fear about speaking in front of the group is to change the focus by asking the children to speak in different ways – for example as quietly as mice, like grumpy bears, very quickly, facing outwards. Keep changing the manner so that the children are too busy concentrating to worry about speaking out.

Round we go

Rounds are useful for encouraging children to speak in a supported way. They have a sentence stem to help them with their speech.

Resources

None

What to do

The children sit in a circle. They take turns around the circle to complete a sentence stem. If children are new to this type of activity, keep the sentence simple – for example 'My favourite food is . . .' With older children, or those more familiar with this sort of activity, try to encourage imaginative thinking by using rounds such as 'The most exciting place to visit would be . . .'

Comments

The children can use a talking object for this game if you prefer. This is a small object that can be easily held in a hand, such as a painted wooden egg. The talking object is held by the child whilst they speak and then passed on to the next child. The rule is that only the child who is holding the object may speak. Discourage any negative responses to the choices children might make during rounds.

Aliens talking

The fun of this game helps children to forget that they are
speaking in front of their peers.

Resources

None

What to do

Divide the children into pairs. Tell each pair to find a space to work
in. Tell them that they are aliens visiting Earth and must conduct
their conversation in an alien language. Tell them to practise their
conversation. They must pay particular attention to their tone of
voice and make sure that it reflects what is being said. They could
also think about the use of gestures and facial expressions. When
the children have practised this, ask for volunteers to perform their
conversations to the group. Ask the group if they could tell what
the conversation was about and what helped them to find this out.

Comments

You could develop this with older children by asking them to write
their own conversations and then 'translate' them into an alien
language. When a pair has performed their conversation, ask the
other children to try to guess what it was about.

Paired poem

This activity encourages children to speak out with the support of a partner.

Resources

A selection of age-appropriate poetry books, one between two if possible

What to do

Sort the children into pairs, with a confident child partnering each shyer child. Give each pair a poetry book. Tell the children to look through their book and find a poem that they both like. Ask the children to read through the poem together a few times and then to practise reading alternate lines or verses. When the children have practised this, ask for volunteers to read their poem to the class.

Comments

If they prefer, very young children can say nursery rhymes that they know.

Spin the bottle

This game provides children with the opportunity to say something in front of a group which they have not prepared.

Resources

Some empty plastic bottles and some prompt cards (see page 135)

What to do

Divide the group into two or three smaller groups. You can put the shyer children into a group with children whom you know will be supportive of them. The groups make their own circles. Put some prompt cards in the centre of each. The children take turns to spin a bottle inside their circle. When the bottle comes to rest, whoever the neck of the bottle is facing says a sentence about themselves. If a child is unable to think of anything to say, they take a prompt card to help them.

Comments

Discuss with the children before they play what they might say. They can pass on information such as age, clubs they belong to and pets they have, or talk about their likes/dislikes. You can also play this game with a topic – for example books or pop groups. When the bottle comes to rest, the child facing the neck says a sentence relating to the topic.

Further activities

Announcements

Write out announcements on cards for different children to make. For example 'Today our key learning objective in literacy is . . .' or 'Later we shall be . . .'

Word association

Play a word association game around the circle. See how fast the children can play the game. Set a target of getting round the whole circle without a break.

Speeches

Ask the children to write out a short speech about something they enjoy doing. Encourage all the children to read out their speeches to the group.

Names in a hat

Use a different approach to asking the children to speak, by pulling names out of a hat. Allow the option to say 'Pass'.

Story round

The children sit in a circle. Each child has to say one word or one sentence to make up a story, going around the circle.

Funny words

Write out some funny-sounding words and say them together. Invite the children to think of some for you all to say – for example higgledy-piggledy, chop-suey, diphthong, Gorgonzola.

Thinking

Children need to learn how to make considered responses, rather than saying the first thing that comes into their heads. The games in this section aim to encourage children to think before they speak.

Be the seeker

Children really enjoy playing this game. Older children love to try to outwit their peers by finding the perfect hiding place.

Resources

A small object

What to do

Decide on a time when you are happy to allow the children 5 minutes to search the room. Before they arrive, hide your object somewhere in the room. When the children arrive, tell them that you have hidden whatever your object is and that they are to find it. Outline all the out-of-bounds areas – for example a store cupboard, anywhere that would necessitate climbing on a chair or table, children's lockers – and before they search for the object discuss the need for respect for property. Allow the children a set time to try to locate the object.

Comments

The children can take turns to hide the object, but always check that its location is suitable before inviting the other children to search for it. You could also hide the object outside in a safe location.

Odd bods

The children can have fun in this game, making strange-looking people and thinking about the most humorous combinations.

Resources

Collect a selection of magazine photographs of people. Cut these into heads, torsos and lower limbs.

What to do

Ask the children to get into pairs. Put the heads, torsos and lower limbs from the magazine photographs into separate piles. Ask the pairs to come forward in turn to choose an item from each of the three piles. Each pair then puts together their pieces of paper to make a person. When the children have done this, allow a couple of minutes for the children to look at each other's creations. Then ask the children to return their magazine pieces to the piles and play the game again.

Comments

A variation on this theme would be to ask the children to try to put the photographs back together correctly. You could play the same game using photographs of animals.

Guess who I am

This game requires the children to think about what they are
going to do and to interpret what they see.

Resources

Brainstorm characters with the children – for example a giant, a
Zulu warrior, a fairy queen, Cat-Woman, Hercules, a mermaid, a king
or queen, Superman. Write a list of these so the children can see it.

What to do

Ask for a volunteer to mime one of the characters from the list for
the others to guess. Tell the children they need to think carefully
about the actions to perform to make sure that they are giving
helpful clues. Once they have performed their mime, ask the other
children to guess who it is. The children can have up to three tries.
If nobody is correct, the child who did the mime says who it was
and a new child is chosen to do a different mime.

Comments

If you think that your group need additional help, the children
could ask questions that require a 'yes' or 'no' answer from the child
after they have done their mime.

Formula 1 quiz

Children have to use their thinking skills and work together
as a team to win the quiz.

Resources

An age-appropriate quiz (see page 136 for a quiz for 8-year-old
children)

What to do

Divide the group into two teams that are evenly matched in ability.
Ask some of the team members quiz questions, making sure each
team is asked the same number of questions. Two points are
awarded for a correct answer, one point if the question is
subsequently answered by the other team. Ask some questions that
are to be answered by the first child to raise their hand (from either
team), again awarding two points for a correct answer.

Comments

An alternative way of scoring is to use a picture of a race track
divided into twenty or so sections and have two cut-out cars, one
for each team. The track could be drawn on a flipchart and the cars
stuck on with Blu-tack. The cars move two sections for a correct
answer and one section if the question is subsequently passed to
and answered correctly by the other team. The winning team is the
first to get their car across the finishing line.

Rhyme and reason

Children apply their experience and knowledge to choosing
suitable words. They spark off ideas from one another.

Resources

A selection of rhyming poems suitable for your group, for example:

Waiting at the Window   Jim
Forgiven   Matilda
– both by A. A. Milne   – both by Hilaire Belloc

You are old, Father William
The Walrus and the Carpenter
– both by Lewis Carroll

Have the original version available. Write out a poem with the
second word of each rhyming couplet erased.

What to do

Put the children into pairs. Explain that you have erased certain
words in a poem and they are going to guess what they are. Tell
them to read through the poem first to get an idea of what it is
about, then go through it again thinking of suitable words to insert
into the spaces. Remind them that the words must rhyme. When
they have finished thinking, ask them to compare the ideas each of
the pairs have had. Read the original poem to the children. If there
were differences in the words used, ask them if they prefer what
they thought of.

Comments

For younger children you could use simpler rhymes or provide three
words for each space and ask them to choose the most suitable.

What am I thinking? (1)

In this game the children have to think about the best way to formulate appropriate questions.

Resources

Category cards (see page 137)

What to do

Divide the children into pairs. The first child in each pair takes a category card from you and thinks of a suitable person or item for the category they have picked. They show the card to their partner, who has to try to guess what the first child thought of by asking questions. Once they guess correctly, they swap roles and return the card. The new category holder then takes a fresh card from you and the game begins again.

Comments

Tell the children that they are not allowed just to make guesses, hoping that they will eventually hit on the correct answer. The child guessing needs to think of appropriate questions that will yield clues to the answer. You can limit the questions to a set number if you want to speed up the proceedings.

What am I thinking? (2)

Children learn the rudiments of categorising in this game.
They need to think carefully about the questions they ask.

Resources

You will need about a dozen small objects to place on a table top –
for example a piece of chalk, a glass, a vase, a pen, a calculator, a
pair of scissors, a paper clip, a ruler, a rubber, an envelope. Try to
have some made of plastic, metal and glass and some of similar
shapes (such as a plastic jug and a plastic cup).

What to do

The children sit in front of the table. Think of one of the objects on
the table. Invite the children to ask five questions to help them
guess what you are thinking about. Encourage them to think of
questions that could eliminate several items – for example 'Is the
object made of metal?', 'Is the object hollow?' Once an object has
been eliminated, it is moved to one side of the table.

It is especially important to think carefully before the fifth question
if there are several possible items left. Once the five questions have
been asked, pick a child to make a guess. If they are correct, return
all the items to the centre of the table, choose a different one and
play the game again. If they are incorrect, allow two more children
a chance to guess; if neither is correct, reveal the identity of the
chosen object and then begin a new round.

Comments

The children might like to take turns at thinking of an item and
answering questions. Ask the child who is choosing to whisper their
choice to you so that you can help them if necessary.

A moment's thought

This simple game gets the children thinking and searching their memories for words.

Resources

A pencil and a piece of paper for each child

What to do

Tell the children that you will say a word and they will have a minute to write down all the words they associate with it. Choose words that will conjure up lots of memories, such as 'seaside', 'circus', 'Christmas'. After the minute, ask for a volunteer to read out their words. See what different words other children have thought of. You could see what was the most commonly chosen word. Repeat the process with a different word.

Comments

With older children you could try some abstract concepts such as 'freedom', 'beauty'. You could also invite the children to suggest words themselves. Put pieces of paper with these words on into a hat and pull them out one at a time for use in the game. Children could sketch items if they do not know how to spell their names or know what they are called.

Hesitation

The children have to think and concentrate in this game. You can increase or decrease the number of claps between contributions to change the pace of the action.

Resources

None

What to do

The children sit in a circle. You choose a category, such as pop stars, sports, sandwich fillings or clothing. One child is chosen to begin. They name an item that fits into the chosen category. All the children clap twice in unison, then the child on the left of the first names another item. The children clap again and the activity proceeds around the circle. An item cannot be named twice. If a child hesitates after the clapping, all the children clap four more times and shout 'Hesitation'. This child then has to begin a new category and play continues.

Comments

It may be a good idea to brainstorm possible categories beforehand to give the children some ideas if they have to choose one. Try to get around the circle without a break in the activity. Once the children have achieved this, see how quickly they can do it.

Opposites attract

Children have to think about pairing possibilities and the questions they could ask that would help them find their partners.

Resources

Some sticky tape and paired cards to stick on the children's backs (see page 138)

What to do

Stick a card on every child's back without their seeing what is printed on it. Explain to the children that they will mingle and look at each other's cards. They must try to find the person who has the opposite word to theirs on their back. Allow a set time, such as 5 minutes, and see how many children have located their partner during it. The children can ask other children to give them clues to the words on their own back. However, those asked must not say the actual word when they answer. For example, if the word was 'rich' they could say 'You have lots of money.' Once a child has worked out their own word, they will be able to locate their partner.

Comments

Before you play this game, establish that the children know what opposites are, and brainstorm those they can think of. Discuss the sorts of clues they could give to help others guess their words. Encourage the children not to tell each other what their words are as that spoils the fun.

Further activities

Set a trail

Devise a set of clues to lead some of the children to other children in the group in an outdoor trail, such as 'Find the child with a scarf on.' Once a child has been found, they are given a clue, such as 'Find someone whose name begins with B', and continue the trail.

Word opposites

Call out an attribute and ask the group to call out the opposite, such as heavy/light, tall/short, rich/poor, hot/cold.

The place I'm thinking of

Designate five areas as different places with written signs – for example the beach, the mountain. Turn your back on the group and play music while they walk around. When the music stops, the children choose areas to run to. Once this is done, you think of an area and call out its name. All the children in that area are out. The game continues until you have a winner.

Consequences

In groups of 6, each child writes on the top of a strip of paper the name of a male character. They fold the paper over and pass it on to the next child, who writes 'met' and the name of a female character. The next child writes 'in' or 'at' and a location, the next 'He said . . . ', the next 'She said . . . .' and the next 'The consequence was . . .' The children pass the paper on once more and then read out what is written. Tell the children they must not write unkind things about anyone in their group or class.

Concentrating

The games in this section apply the combined skills of listening, looking, speaking and thinking to activities that encourage concentration. The focus is on paying attention in order to participate successfully.

Look at you

In this game children need to watch carefully in order to copy others and to think about devising a suitable movement.

Resources

None

What to do

The children stand in a circle. Think of a simple series of actions – for example stretching your arms up above your head, lowering them again, then stretching them out to the side and bringing them back. Repeat this series of actions while the children sing (to the tune of 'This old man . . .'):

Look at you, copy you, see what action you can do.
With a nick nack paddy whack, give the dog a chew.
We can do those actions too.

While the children sing the verse, they copy the actions. Choose a child or ask for a volunteer to perform a new series of actions for the children to copy.

Comments

With older children, you can walk behind as they sing and tap someone who is to change the action in the middle of the verse. The children have to be especially vigilant and ready to change their actions.

Letter-box

In this fast-moving game the children must listen and be ready for action.

Resources

An object to place in the centre of the circle. Letters of the alphabet printed on cards (you need all the letters to cover the initials of the first name of every child in the class) placed in a container. Make sure you have plenty of space for this game.

What to do

The children sit in a circle. You say 'Anyone with a name beginning with . . . ', and call out a letter that you take out of the container. All the children that fit into that category stand up and run around the circle in a clockwise direction. When they arrive back at their places, they enter the circle and try to pick up the object. The child who picks up the object pulls out the next letter from the container and calls it. Make sure that the letters are kept out of the container after each turn.

Comments

You can add to the fun by allowing the child who is calling out the letter to decide how the children will move around the outside of the circle – for example hopping, crawling, skipping. They must say the movement before they call out the letter.

Bouncy ball

The children need to watch, listen and be ready to move
when their number is called.

Resources

A ball and sticky labels with numbers on for younger children. You
need some space to play this game.

What to do

Number the children randomly around the circle. If you think they
will forget their numbers, give them sticky labels to wear on their
sleeves. Call out a number and bounce the ball in the centre of the
circle. The child with that number runs into the centre and tries to
catch the ball before it bounces a second time. The child bounces or
throws the ball back to you and the game continues.

Comments

If the children are competent with their ball skills, they can bounce
the ball and call out the numbers.

Surfing

Younger children especially enjoy the anticipation of being chosen in this exciting game.

Resources

None. Plenty of space is needed for this game.

What to do

The children stand in a circle, well spaced out to allow the others to move in and out of the circle. A child is chosen to be the surfer. They weave in and out, between the standing children. As they do this, all the children say together:

Up and down the waves I surf, in and out the sea.
I've a surfboard big and strong, come and ride with me.

At the end of the verse, the child nearest the surfer mimes stepping onto the surfboard behind the first child. They hold onto the first child's waist. The pair then continue in and out of the circle while the children say the verse again. Gradually more and more children join the surfer until there are up to ten children in the line.

Comments

As children leave the circle, ask the remainder to spread out to keep the spaces even.

Don't you dare laugh!

Children have to use all their powers of concentration to try
to keep a straight face in this game.

Resources

None

What to do

The children mill around the room. Each time two children meet,
they take turns to pull a silly face and say in a silly voice 'Don't you
dare laugh!' Any child who does laugh is out and must sit down. The
children continue in this way for several minutes or until only one
person is left.

Comments

Older children can think of amusing things to say to others to try to
make them laugh, such as 'Did you know bees have sticky hair
because they use honeycombs?'

The octopus' treasure

This is a fast action game that keeps the children watchful
and alert as they try to capture the prize.

Resources

Some fish cut out of card, about 50 cm long. The children could
make them in an art lesson.

What to do

The children stand in a circle. A child is chosen to be the octopus
and stand in the middle of the circle. This child places the fish in a
circle around them (about 1.5 metres away). On your command the
children enter the playing area and try to get a fish. If they are
touched by the octopus, they are out. After several turns, see who
has caught the most fish. Play again with a new octopus.

Comments

You can vary the game by putting the children into different
categories – for example fishermen, sharks, mermaids – and calling
one category at a time to play. Another variation is to use pieces of
gold paper, representing treasure and worth varying amounts of
points. The children then have to try to be selective about what
they grab.

Fast forward

Children enjoy the fun of trying to get the actions right at
breakneck speed in this energetic game.

Resources

None

What to do

The children stand in a circle. As you say the following verse, they
perform the actions:

> *Shake head, touch ears, flap arms, twitch nose.*
> *Raise shoulders, knock knees, turn round, tip toes.*
> *Jump twice, touch the ground.*
> *Stretch up high, then lie down.*

Once the children have mastered the verse, speed up the actions
each time. Alternatively, each time you say the verse instead of
mentioning an action leave silence, during which the children must
perform the missing action. Leave an additional action out each
time.

Comments

Hold a knock-out competition to see who is the fastest player in the
class. Each time you speed up, anyone who makes a mistake or
cannot keep up is out.

Racing tableaux

In this game time is limited, so the children have to concentrate and work cooperatively to produce a satisfactory result.

Resources

None

What to do

Divide the class into groups of 6. Explain to them that you will give them each a title and they will have just 2 minutes to arrange themselves into a scene that corresponds to that title. Each member of the group must have a valid role in the scene. Tell the children that the success of their group tableaux will depend on their working well together. Examples of titles are the funfair, the wedding, the ski slope, a party. Inform the children that at the end of 2 minutes they must have taken up their respective positions in the scene. You will shout 'Stop' and they must freeze. At that point ask one member of the group to come out of the scene and describe it to the other groups.

Comments

Try to vary the mood of each tableaux. Discuss with the children afterwards what the most difficult aspect of this activity was, and what the best way of working together was.

The rainbow game

The children need to concentrate on the colours called out in this game to see if they are involved in the action.

Resources

None

What to do

The children sit in a circle. Name the children around the circle, using the colours of the rainbow – red, orange, yellow, green, blue, indigo and violet. Call out one to three different colours. The children representing those colours change places. When you call 'Rainbow', all the children change places.

Comments

To make the children more vigilant, tell them that the last two children to be seated after a change will be out.

Clockwise, anti-clockwise

Children need to concentrate and think about what they
are doing to keep the actions travelling round the circle at
the same pace.

Resources

None

What to do

Send two different actions around the circle at the same time – for
example squeeze the hand of the child on the left to travel in a
clockwise direction and tap the elbow of the child on the right to
travel in an anti-clockwise direction. The object of the game is to
have both actions arrive back with you at the same time.

Comments

Warn the children that they must not pass on an action before they
have received it. They must watch how the actions are travelling
around the circle and synchronise their speeds. With experience,
children could begin the actions for each round.

Further activities

Amoebae

Children form groups of 5. The groups stand in an outward-facing circle and link arms. They decide on a direction and try to move slowly towards their goal.

Twenty

Children play in groups of 3 to 5. In turn, they say a number, starting with 1 and progressively adding on a number from 1 to 5. The object of the game is to try to make another player say 20.

Stuck to the ground

You need a large, soft ball. Four players spread out and can pass the ball between themselves, but cannot move. The other children run around. The four players stuck to the ground must try to hit other children with the ball. These children then become stuck to the ground too and help to get the others stuck. The game continues until all the children are stuck, or you feel they are tiring.

In the hen house

Choose one child to be the fox. The fox stands to one side. The children mill around. Explain that while you count to 3 they are to get into groups of 3 and form a hen in a coop. Two children stand with raised arms, holding hands, while the third shelters underneath. The children are safe in this position. After you have counted to 3, count to 10. During this count any child who is not a sheltering hen or part of a coop can be caught by the fox. Any children caught by the fox before you reach 10 become foxes themselves. Warn the children that even if they are in groups of 3, they are not safe until they are in position.

Thinking of others

This section looks at various aspects of thinking about other people. It focuses on activities that encourage kindness and consideration towards others, and also looks at important skills associated with positive relationships – such as being able to read body language and learn appropriate behaviour by watching others.

The bad bear rap

The children can have fun with this rap whilst thinking about an important aspect of behaviour.

Resources

None

What to do

Read the children the following verses. They can join in the chorus, saying it loudly and clapping to the beat.

Now this is the story of the bad-mannered bear
Who hadn't any manners and just didn't care.
He said: 'I don't mind my p's or my q's,
Cos I do what I want and I say what I choose.'

Chorus

Hey bear, listen bear,
It's not right that you don't care.
Bad mood, mean dude,
We feel you're rude.

He talked all through mealtimes with a mouthful of food,
He dribbled and he belched even though it was rude.
He rocked on his chair, wiped his mouth on his sleeves,
And never said a 'thank you' or even a 'please'.

Chorus

He was mean to the girls and worse to the boys.
He pushed and he bullied and he wouldn't share his toys.

He didn't help anyone or clean up his mess,
And if anyone should nag him, why he'd do even less.

Chorus

He talked over others when he should have been quiet
But he never said 'good morning' and never said 'good night'.
He threw down his sweet wrappers straight on the floor,
And he always kicked open, then slammed, every door.

Chorus

We've had enough of you now, bad-mannered bear.
Your behaviour is appalling and it just isn't fair.
So take yourself away and learn what is right.
We'd like you back when you can be polite.

Comments

Remind the children that you don't want any bad-mannered bears in your group.

Kindness calling

Role-playing events in which the children are considering the feelings of others give the children an opportunity to think about and discuss the emotions engendered by being kind and also by receiving kindness.

Resources

A flipchart and marker pen

What to do

Brainstorm and record on the flipchart a selection of events that encourage kindness – for example a child falls over and is hurt, a child loses something precious, a child has a row with a family member, a child is feeling unwell.

Put the children into groups of 3. Give them a scenario to discuss and then ask them to practise acting it out. They can take turns at playing the various roles. Ask if any group would like to show their scene to the other groups. Afterwards, talk to the children about being kind. Ask them how it feels to be kind to others and how it feels when someone is kind to them. Ask the children if they can think of the reasons why they are sometimes unkind, but do not let them name any children. Ask them if they can think of anything that might help them to be kind in such situations.

Comments

You could ask the children to brainstorm different occasions when someone might feel sad and need to receive kindness from others. This could be helpful in highlighting areas of concern.

Afloat in a boat

This is a game for creating good feeling in the group. There is an added spark of anticipation in the guessing part.

Resources

A small object to pass around the circle

What to do

The children sit in a circle. They pass the object round and say:

> [The number of children in the circle] *were afloat in a boat,*
> *There was a loud shout and one fell out.*

Whoever is holding the object on the word 'out' moves to sit in the middle of the circle. The game continues, reducing the number of children by one each time. However, the children who are out have an opportunity to get back into the boat again. Before the next round, they each say who they think will be out next time. If a child is correct, they swap places with that child and return to the boat. If more than one child guesses correctly, you chose which of them swaps places.

Comments

The children guessing who might be out next must do so quickly. Do not allow them time to try to work it out against the rhyme. Remember to adjust the number if someone gets back in the boat. Continue until the game is no longer viable.

Dining out

This interesting game can lead to all sorts of discussions, such as eating healthy foods, foods from other countries.

Resources

Menus written by the children (these should include main meals, puddings, drinks and side orders, all numbered), tablecloths, cutlery, plastic plates, bowls and cups. Pencils and small pads for the waiters and waitresses.

What to do

Divide the children into groups of 4 or 5. Explain to them that they are going to role play dining out at a restaurant. One child will be a waiter or waitress and the others will be diners. They must first set the scene by laying a table. The diners can be a family or friends. They must study the menu, order food from the waiter or waitress and mime eating it when it arrives. The waiter must write down each person's order (this can be done as numbers to make it easier) and then mime bringing food to the table and clearing it away once the diners have finished. The children must pay particular attention to the manner in which they speak to each other. Exchanges between the diners and waiter must be polite. Encourage the children to think about their mealtime conversations. Allow the children 5 minutes to plan their role play. Ask if any groups wish to show what they have done to the other groups.

Comments

Make sure that children have a chance to play different roles within the scene. Ask the children for their views on eating out. What do they like/dislike about it? Where is their favourite place and why?

Crosspatch, put up the latch

This game provides a lead into discussion about anger and being bad tempered. You can also use it to help the children think about the similarities and differences between people.

Resources

None. You need plenty of space to play in.

What to do

A child is chosen to be Crosspatch and stand at one end of the room. The other children stand at the opposite end. The children call to Crosspatch:

> *Crosspatch, put up the latch, you can be nice if you try.*
> *It's rainy and cold, we're soaking wet. We want to come in and get dry.*
> Crosspatch answers the children in the following way:
> *I can only be a little bit nice, so anyone with* [category] *can take . . . steps.*

Crosspatch names a category – for example anyone who has a cat, a T in their name, size 2 shoes, brown eyes – and says how many steps they are to take. Repeat the process with Crosspatch choosing a different category and number of steps. The first child to reach Crosspatch takes that place and the game begins again.

Comments

Talk to the children about how they feel when someone is cross with them. What things do they do to help themselves and the situation? Talk to them also about what makes them cross, but do not allow them to name individuals.

Reactions

This game focuses on reading body language for clues about how a person is reacting.

Resources

A headband, either one made of elasticated material or one that fastens with Velcro. A selection of nouns written on cards that you can attach to the headband so that the wearer cannot see what is written on them. Examples are man-eating tiger, tooth fairy, bad-tempered bear, giant, kitten.

What to do

The children sit in a circle. Choose a volunteer to wear the headband. Attach one of the cards to the front by tucking it under the elastic or using a Velcro pad. The others then volunteer to act in a way that gives the wearer clues to their identity. The child who is guessing can ask questions that require a 'yes' or 'no' answer. The children can also say something to give a clue, but it must not contain the actual word(s) shown. The children raise their hands if they want to participate, and wait to be chosen. When a correct guess has been made, another child has a turn with a different card.

Comments

Encourage the children not to put up their hands until they have thought about how they would react or what they would say, to avoid long delays in the activity. If someone seems to be stuck you can give them a clue.

The third way

This game focuses on the skills of negotiation and
compromise and shows the children that there are always
options other than conflict.

Resources

A list of confrontational dilemmas listed on a flipchart – for
example two children want the same toy; two children blame each
other for starting a fight; three children want to watch different TV
programmes at the same time; one child wants a third child to join
in a game but the second child does not; one child wants to tell the
teacher about a child who has done something wrong, but another
child does not.

What to do

Put the children into pairs and give each pair a dilemma from the
list. Ask each pair to put their dilemma into a context that will show
the group how the quarrel began. They must then work together to
decide on a solution that is as fair as possible for all of the children
in the scenario. When the children have had about 15 minutes to
work through their task, call them into a circle to discuss the
solutions that they have thought of. Ask children why they think
people quarrel and what the hardest part of finding an amicable
solution is.

Comments

Ask the children to watch television especially carefully and to
notice what people generally quarrel about. Talk to the children
about how they think these quarrels could be avoided.

Catch the clap

This is an action copying game played at speed. Everyone has to remain alert and be ready to respond as they never know when it will be their turn.

Resources

None

What to do

The children stand in a circle. Begin the game by performing a simple action – for example crouch down and touch the floor. The children clap twice, then you name and point to a child. This child has to copy the action. They then think of a new action that they show to the others in the group. The children again clap twice and the performer names and points to another child. The play continues like this. The children have to follow the actions around the circle as they change each time. The aim is to have no hesitation in the flow of the game, so each child must be ready to perform as soon as the two claps have taken place.

Comments

As the children become familiar with the activity, you can speed up the claps and make the movements more complex.

A positive influence

This is an opportunity for everyone in the class to give and receive positive thoughts and feel good about themselves and others.

Resources

Enough pairs of scissors for one pair per child in your group and a photocopied list of ten positive statements for each child. Examples are: you are always kind, you have a lovely smile, you always work hard, you are very friendly, you are a very tidy person, you have very neat writing. Make sure there is a list for every child in the class. These could be built up beforehand over a number of Circle Times.

What to do

Give each child their sheet of positive statements and divide the children into groups of 6. Tell them that they must choose a positive statement from their lists to give to each member of their group. The children then cut up their sheets and distribute the statements. They must not discuss this with the other children, but must make their own personal choices. When everyone has received all their statements, call the children into a circle. Talk to them about how they feel to read positive comments about themselves. Did the children receive a variety of statements or did they receive several of the same kind?

Comments

You can use this activity to remind the children in the future about how they felt to receive positive statements and how different it feels to receive unkind comments.

Spies and spycatchers

This is an exciting game that requires the children to study body language for clues.

Resources

Enough small cards for each child in the group to have one. On six of the cards print 'S' for spy. On three of the cards print 'C' for catcher and on four of the cards print 'D' for decoy. Leave the remaining cards blank.

What to do

Explain to the children what is on the cards and give them out. Warn the children that they must not let anyone see what is on their card, even if it is blank. Divide the room into two halves. Tell the children they must all mingle in one half of the room. The object of the game is for the spies to reach the far end of the other half of the room without being caught by a spycatcher. The spies and catchers have to try to disguise who they are by not making their behaviour too obvious. When a spy thinks they are safe, they make a dash for the far wall. The decoys are there to fool the spies and catchers by pretending that they are either spies or catchers and behaving in an obvious way, such as showing that they are looking for an opportunity to escape or pretending to look for the spies. However, the decoys cannot leave their half of the room, nor can the other children with blank cards leave that half – the latter must mingle without pretending to be anything. When all the spies have tried to escape, collect in the cards and start again.

Comments

Discuss with the children the body language clues they looked for to identify the characters.

Further activities

Good manners

Brainstorm with the children all the things that they consider to be good manners. Have a weekly focus on one of them and reward those children who try really hard to reflect it in their behaviour.

Manners board

Have an on-going board on which points awarded to children can be recorded, or which children can move up if they receive a commendation for having good manners from any adult. Make sure that all children receive some recognition over time.

My special day

Have a 'My special day' for each child, when they have the opportunity of receiving a special positive focus.

Circle Time

Use Circle Time to promote positive behaviour and help individuals receive group support in an action plan. (See the Training and resources section for more details.)

Special treat

Allow the children to choose a special treat, for having tried really hard to maintain good behaviour and think of others.

Anger strategies

Brainstorm with the children all the helpful ways of trying to keep their tempers – for example counting slowly to 10, thinking of a positive experience.

Working together

The games in this section allow children to appreciate the benefits of working together. They are able to see that by pooling their mental and physical resources they can achieve an objective more easily and efficiently than individually. They will also find it enjoyable to have the company of others whilst they are working.

A pair of hands

This is a gentle, relaxing activity that gives the children an opportunity to discuss their ideas with a partner.

Resources

Paper and pencils

What to do

Put the children into pairs. Each pair needs two pieces of paper and two pencils. The children take it in turns to lay their hands, side by side, fingers outstretched and palms down, on a piece of paper for their partner to draw around. The children then write details about themselves on each of the ten digits – for example name, age, siblings, pets, what they want to be when they grow up, favourite colour, favourite pastime, favourite meal, best film, where they would like to spend a day with their partner.

Comments

You can either display a hand with details on it so that all the children work to the same format or discuss possible items and then let each pair talk through and choose their own categories.

The elevator

This game relies on cooperation and trust between partners. Both children in each pair have to work equally hard to achieve a result.

Resources

None

What to do

Put the children into pairs. Ask them to stand back to back with their partner and link arms. They are going to try to sit down gently and carefully without letting go of their partner's arms. Once they have achieved this, they are going to stand, again without letting go of their partner's arms.

Comments

Try to pair children of similar height. Warn them that they must not be silly in this activity as you do not want any children to sit down heavily and risk hurting themselves.

Get into the right suits

This activity requires concentration and cooperation. The
competitive element adds to the fun.

Resources

A pack of playing cards

What to do

You will need an equal number of each of the four suits to give
every child in the class a card. Explain to the children that you will
give them each a card. On your command, they must look at their
cards and then, in silence, find all the other children with cards of
the same suit. When they have achieved this, they must arrange
themselves in a line, one behind the other and in height order,
shortest at the front and tallest at the back. As soon as they have
done this, they can sit down to show that they have finished. The
first suit to sit in the correct order is the winner.

Comments

If you have a number of children that does not fit exactly into the
four suits, any remaining can be marshals and watch over the
proceedings. After the first game, the marshals swap places with
other children. Collect in the cards, shuffle and deal them again to
start a new game.

Picture perfect

Children swap creative ideas and work together to produce a picture, using shapes in an imaginative way.

Resources

Paper and pencils, photocopied shapes page (see page 139)

What to do

Divide the class into pairs or small groups. Give each group a shapes page and paper and pencils. Ask them to create a picture that incorporates all the shapes. They can add things to the shapes, but not change them. They can also include other items to enhance their pictures. After 10 minutes call the groups back to the circle to show their pictures.

Comments

Another activity is to choose one shape for the children and ask them to see how many different things they can turn it into.

Whom am I talking about?

This game stimulates thinking and discussion as the children work together as a team.

Resources

Paper and two pencils

What to do

Divide the children into two teams. Tell the teams to go to opposite ends of the room and to talk quietly so that the other team does not overhear them. Each team needs to elect a scribe who is good at writing. The scribe lists the names of the children in their team. Each child then volunteers an interesting fact about themselves that the scribe notes beside the appropriate name. These could include an unusual hobby, an interesting possession, somewhere special they have visited, something unusual about where they live. Encourage the children to think of something that is not common knowledge. One child introduces three of their team-mates by name to the other team and then says 'One of these people . . .', choosing the fact that relates to one of them. The other team has to decide which child the fact relates to. If their guess is correct, they get a point. The teams take turns to introduce three of their team-mates and to guess the children the other team's facts relate to, with different children taking the different roles each time.

Comments

Ask the teams to help those children who might find it difficult to think of an interesting fact about themselves by giving suggestions that they think would be useful.

How long will it take?

This game requires children to cooperate as they discuss and reach a realistic decision about who is most representative of the majority.

Resources

Two stopwatches, paper and two pencils. Enough space to run around in freely is needed.

What to do

Divide the group into two teams. The teams stand at one end of the room. Explain to them that they must choose one person who is most representative of them at running. They do not want the fastest or the slowest as overall time is what is important. Impress on the children that this is not a race. The chosen child must run to the far wall and back whilst being timed with a stopwatch. Based on this time, the children must estimate how quickly their whole team can complete the run, one at a time. Each team writes down their estimate. On your command, the teams begin to run in turn and you start the stopwatches, one for each team. You stop each team's stopwatch when its members have completed their run and are sitting down. The teams get one point if they are inside their estimated time and the team that is nearest to the estimate gets an additional point.

Comments

Try this with different activities, such as traditional races, hopping, walking backwards, doing twenty skips, performing a routine in turn, putting something together.

Balloon blowing

The children need to work together to try to win this game.

Resources

A blown-up balloon, a piece of string or a chalk line. You need enough space to play the game safely.

What to do

Divide the class into two teams. The teams line up facing each other, about 4 metres apart. They get down on their hands and knees. Halfway between the two teams, draw a chalk line or stretch out the string along the ground. Place the balloon on the line between the two teams. Then draw two lines each 1 metre either side of the centre line, or use some more string. This marks each team's area, which they must remain inside. The children have to work together to try to blow the balloon into the other team's area. Allow them a minute, then stop the game. No-one must continue blowing or a penalty point will be given to the other team. Award a point to the successful team. When the children have had a short rest, begin again.

Comments

Each time you start a session, pull the children back to their original positions as they will gradually shuffle forwards. They must not cross the line into the other team's area.

Eel-ongated

This is a fast, active game that is great fun to play. The children have to work together to try to increase the number of children in their team.

Resources

None. Plenty of space to run around is needed.

What to do

Divide the children into three equal teams and ask the teams to spread out in the playing area. If any children are left over, they can be observers. The children in each team line up one behind the other and hold the waist of the child in front. Tell the teams that they are three eels swimming in the sea. The object of the game is to grow longer by 'eating' other children. The child at the front of the line must put his hands on the waist of the child at the end of another team's line. This child must then let go and become the new head of the catcher's eel. The children have to try to increase the number of children in their line, whilst protecting their own tail. Give them a few minutes to play, then call a halt and see which team has the longest eel. Start again with new teams, including any observers by getting children who have already played to swap with them.

Comments

You could allow the teams 5 minutes at the start of the lesson to practise moving together. Discuss what tactics the teams employed and what methods of moving together efficiently they found.

Starcatcher

This is an active game that encourages children to work together to achieve their goals.

Resources

None. Plenty of room to run about in is needed.

What to do

Tell the children that they are lights floating in the night sky. Choose one child to be the Starcatcher. The Starcatcher stands in the centre and the lights move around them. You will say 'Lights to star bright. 1, 2, 3, 4, 5.' The lights have to get into groups of 5. They form stars by putting their left hands together in the centre of a circle and stretching out their right arms like the rays of a star. On the number 5, the Starcatcher tries to catch any spare lights that are floating about by touching them on the shoulder. The Starcatcher may do this only during a second count to 5. Any lights that are caught become Starcatchers as well, and the game continues. The Starcatchers work together to try to corner spare lights and the stars work together by trying to distract the Starcatchers.

Comments

You can speed up or slow down the numbers counted to help the lights or the Starcatchers.

Interior designer

The children use their experience and imaginations to work
together to think of a practical and attractive design.

Resources

You can do this activity as a two- or three-dimensional project. You
will need appropriate resources of paper, colours, cardboard boxes
and other craft materials for the approach you and the group decide
to take.

What to do

Divide the children into small groups of 3 or 4. Explain to them that
you want them to design their ideal classroom. They can choose the
shape, colours and fittings such as seating arrangements and work
surfaces. Discuss with the children the requirements of a classroom
and the practicalities they will need to consider. Give them time to
discuss the project and to decide on the way they would like to
approach it. Allow a reasonable amount of time for the development
of their ideas. Later, let each group show their design to the other
groups and talk through the choices they have made.

Comments

Have fun by asking the children to say what they think a classroom
will be like in fifty years time. Encourage them to be imaginative
and fanciful.

Further activities

Animal magic

Put the children into groups of 5 or 6. Give each group an animal and ask them to brainstorm reasons why their animal is the best in the world. They could use library or computer resources. Allow each group to share their findings with the other groups.

Word sculpture

Divide the group into three teams. Call out simple words such as 'cat' and 'dog' and ask the teams to make body sculptures of the letters forming each word, or the object itself. Have a race to see which team can make a word in the fastest time.

Team flags

If your organisation has teams or houses, ask the children to design a flag for the one they belong to. Discuss with them the qualities they would like it to possess and ask them to think of items that could represent this – for example a bee might show being busy, a rock might show steadfastness.

Team quizzes

Put the children into mixed-ability teams and let each team devise a quiz for another team, using their own knowledge. Discuss with them things they might ask questions about, such as books, pop stars.

Group challenges

Devise some challenges that the children can do in groups, such as complete a jigsaw or another puzzle, build an obstacle course from a set number of items, build something from scrap materials.

Enhancing communication skills

This section combines the skills of listening and speaking in activities that focus on knowing how and when to respond. These are important skills for children to learn to help them to appraise situations and behave in socially appropriate ways.

Missing letters

The children need to listen carefully and concentrate in order
to play this game. If they are not fully focused, they may fail
to respond in the correct manner.

Resources

None

What to do

The children sit in a circle. A child is chosen to begin the game.
They say the first letter of the alphabet. The child on their left then
says the next letter, and this continues around the circle. When the
group reach the end of the alphabet, ask them to say it again,
leaving out certain letters. Match this to the age or ability of the
group – for example they might be asked to leave out a, e, i, o and
u. The children have to remember the omitted letters. Discuss
pictures that the children could associate with each letter to assist
their memories. If a child's turn coincides with one of the chosen
letters, they must omit that letter and say the next letter in the
sequence. Any child who gets this wrong is out. When one child is
out, begin the game again without that child, leaving out different
letters. Continue the game until you have one child left.

Comments

You can vary the pace of the game and the number of letters you
omit according to the age and ability of the players.

The shop game

This activity uses a game format to show the children how to ask for items in a polite manner.

Resources

A set of shop cards (see page 140)

What to do

The children sit in a circle. If you think it is necessary, brainstorm all the shops that they can think of and what each type sells. Tell the children that for the purposes of the game, the shops involved will sell only the items suggested by their names – for example, the jeweller will sell only jewellery and watches, not gifts and so on. One child is chosen to be the shopkeeper, and selects a card without letting the other children see what is on it. The shopkeeper stands in the centre of the circle. Other children volunteer to enter the shop, one at a time, to make a purchase. They must say 'Please may I have . . .' If the item is not stocked in the shop, the shopkeeper answers 'I'm sorry, Sir/Madam, I don't sell . . .' The customer then has an opportunity to make two more requests in their attempt to guess what sort of shop it is. If the item is available, the shopkeeper says 'Certainly, Sir/Madam' and mimes handing the item over. After three sales have been confirmed, the children in the circle then have up to three opportunities to guess what the shop is. If the shop is not guessed correctly, the shopkeeper reveals what sort of shop it is. The game begins again with a new shopkeeper.

Comments

Do not allow the children to make random guesses. They need to have three sales confirmed before they make an attempt.

Talking choices

This activity focuses on the various voices we use to talk to different people. The children will have fun, laughing at their choices.

Resources

A list of characters that you draw up yourself or ask the children to brainstorm with you on a flipchart. Examples are a toddler, a clown, an elderly person, an artist, a police officer, a friend, a next-door neighbour.

What to do

Ask the group to sit in a circle. Tell the children that they are going to pretend that different characters come into their garden and take their ball. The gist of what they have to say is 'Excuse me, I think you've taken my ball. May I please have it back.' Choose one of the characters from the list and ask a volunteer to show how they would address that person. Discuss with the other children if they agree with this approach. If they do not, ask them why. When the children have agreed, they can ask for the ball back together. Continue with a different character.

Comments

Ask the children to think of how they could say 'Please leave me alone to read quietly' to a fire-breathing dragon.

Short scenes

In this game the children use their experience to focus on
the language they would use in a given situation.

Resources

A list of different scenarios written on a flipchart, such as taking an
animal to the vet, visiting a doctor, going to the hairdresser, buying
a book, ordering a meal in a restaurant

What to do

Put the children into small groups of 3 or 4. Give each group a
scenario and ask them to make up a short scene involving all the
children as different characters. Tell the children to pay particular
attention to the language they use to try to make the scene
realistic. When the groups have practised, let them each perform
their scenario for the others.

Comments

Talk to the children about how they knew what to include in their
characters' lines. Discuss with them how we pick up information by
talking to, reading about and watching others.

The right location

Good communication skills include the ability to listen well
to what others are saying to you. This activity focuses on
that ability.

Resources

Label up to eight different areas around the edges of the room.
These might include a wood, a beach, a mountain, a lakeside, a
park, a jungle. You will need space for the children to run around in.

What to do

The children mime playing in the middle of the room, while you say:

> All the children were playing one day.
> Along came an ogre and chased them away.
> 'Where shall we hide?' they asked as they fled.
> 'Go to . . . ,' their teacher said.

As soon as the teacher names the location, the children run to that
place. The last two to reach it are out. Continue the game, naming
different locations, until one child is left. They are the winner.

Comments

The children will probably want to join in with the rhyme once they
know it, but they must be quiet when you name the location or
some children may not hear it.

Catch the fox

This is another game that calls for careful listening. A slow response may mean that a child is out.

Resources

A story, poem or set of instructions. Plenty of space for the children to run about in.

What to do

Sort the children into groups of 3. Any spare children are hunters; if there are no spares, choose one group to play that role. The hunters stand around the edge of the room and the groups of 3 stand in the middle. One child in each group becomes a fox. The two remaining children stand on either side of the fox and join hands around them, providing a lair. The children must listen for the cue words 'foxes on the prowl'. Read the chosen text to them, inserting in it from time to time the cue words. As soon as you speak these words, all the foxes must leave their lairs and find new ones. The hunters can catch any fox out of a lair by touching them on the shoulder. They then reverse roles for the next game.

Comments

Talk with the children about all the things we can learn from listening carefully to others.

What can the animals do?

This activity encourages the children to put their thoughts into words and communicate these to others.

Resources

None

What to do

The children say the following verse together:

Today we are all going to the zoo.
We want to see what the animals can do.
We'll look in the pens and enclosures too
And then we'll know what the animals do.

Choose an animal and ask the children to volunteer information about it. For example, if you choose a snake the children may say the following:

I'm a snake and I can slither.
I'm a snake and I have scales.
I'm a snake and I can hiss.
I'm a snake and I'm yellow and black.

After you have chosen a few children to give information, say the verse again and pick a different animal.

Comments

As a variation, you could ask the children to choose an animal each time.

Noah's ark

This game encourages the children to participate in communicating ideas.

Resources

A list on a flipchart of the animals for Noah to consult with

What to do

Ask the children to suggest a mime for each animal. For example:

monkey – bend knees, stick out bottom and hang arms near the ground

elephant – wave arm in front of face like trunk

giraffe – stretch arms and reach as high as you can

snake – lie down on the ground.

Choose a child to be Noah. They go to the other end of the room and turn their back on the children. They say to the children 'Choose which animal you want to be.' When each child has decided on an animal they call to Noah:

Noah, Noah, it's raining and dark.
Let us come inside your ark.

After studying the mimes Noah guesses one or more of the animals and tells them how many steps they can move forward. The game continues with the children choosing a different animal each round until one of the animals reaches the end and touches Noah. This child becomes the new Noah and the game starts again.

Comments

Make sure that children do not change their animal after Noah has spoken.

Talk back

This game focuses the children's attention on the idea that we communicate with people in different ways depending on their status and the circumstances.

Resources

A flipchart and marker pen

What to do

Make two lists on the flipchart to represent people that the children would talk to in a formal way – such as a teacher, doctor, police officer, shop assistant – and those they talk to in an informal way – such as friends, family members, other children. Explore with the children what they think are the reasons why they talk formally to certain people. Discuss with them how they know when to talk formally or informally. Ask them what would happen if they got it wrong.

Comments

This activity could lead to a discussion about how we behave appropriately in different circumstances and how we learn the correct behaviour.

Trios

This is a fun activity that encourages children to communicate effectively in order to find the other members of their groups.

Resources

Trios cards (see page 141)

What to do

Explain to the children that you are going to distribute sets of cards. Each set contains three cards. One card states an item and the other two are sentences relating to the item. Shuffle the cards well and deal them out to the children. Tell them not to show their cards to any other children. When the game begins they must mingle and ask each other questions relating to the statements on their cards until they have found the other members of their group. When they have done this, they sit down.

Comments

Discuss the nature of the questions the children might ask. Then encourage the children to spend a minute thinking about specific questions they might ask, given the information on their cards.

Further activities

Minute talks

Ask the children to prepare a talk that lasts for a minute. This can either be about themselves or a topic that interests them.

Five facts

Put the children into groups of 2 or 3. Have a list of animals or other topics ready and ask them to use the library or internet facilities at their disposal to find out five interesting facts about one of the things on the list.

Modes of communication

Look at some unusual ways of communicating with the children, such as Morse code, sign language, flags, smoke signals.

Secret codes

Ask the children to think up secret codes in pairs and write letters to their partner. Give them some ideas, such as substituting numbers for letters, using symbols, moving letters along.

Chatterbox

Ask the children to prepare a speech about any subject of their choice. Using a stopwatch, time each child to see who can speak the longest without hesitation or repetition.

Showtime

Let the children devise a show in which everybody is involved in some way. Children can read poetry, sing a song and so on. Those children who do not want to perform can be the announcers.

Skills for out and about

This section focuses on a range of social skills that children need in their lives outside school or the particular group that you are connected with. Some of these involve personal competence as an aid to independence and others are important in forming positive relationships with others.

Holidays

The following four games are based on a holiday theme. The first activity requires group cooperation and planning skills.

Resources

You will need to make up four posters advertising holiday destinations, using cut-up magazines or holiday brochures. The first poster advertises a luxury hotel in a woodland setting – Badgerwood Hotel, ideal for peace and quiet and beautiful walks. The second place, Clifftops, has self-catering chalet houses and provides an all-action sports holiday with rock climbing, abseiling, horse riding and so on. The third, Fun Palace at Lower Westway, is a caravan site with entertainment halls, swimming pool, amusement arcades and fast-food bars. The fourth is Seaview, a coastal resort with sandy beaches, blue sea and guest houses.

What to do

Divide the group into sets of 4 to 6. Tell them that each group represents a family who have to choose a holiday destination. Show them the four posters and talk about what they would find and what they could do at each of the destinations. They must then decide where they would like to go. They must make a list of everything they would need to pack to take on their holiday. They must think about how they would get to the station – for example would they need to book a taxi? When the groups have organised their holiday, call them into a circle to discuss their plans.

Comments

Talk to the children about holidays they have had. What do they most enjoy doing when they are away? How do their families prepare to go away?

Get packing

This is an enjoyable team game that is based on the holiday theme and children organising themselves.

Resources

Three similar, medium-sized cardboard boxes with lids (an additional piece of card will be fine) from a supermarket to represent suitcases. A selection of items brought in, or made from art materials, to be packed in these suitcases. Let the children suggest the items the day before you intend to play the game – for example trainers, jumpers, sun cream, bucket and spade, swimming costumes. You will need three sets of similar items. The idea is to have enough items to fill the boxes to capacity, so that they need fairly careful packing to fit everything in and close the lid.

What to do

The children are divided into three teams. They line up at one end of the room with their suitcases. The items to be packed are placed at the other end of the room. On the command 'Go', the first member of each team runs to the far end of the room, selects an item, runs back with it and places it in the suitcase. The child returns to the end of their line and the second child in their team repeats the process. The children continue like this until all the items have been packed in their case and the lid is closed. The first team to finish with a carefully packed case is the winner.

Comments

It is a good idea to let the children try packing the cases before the game. They must finish with the lid closed. If all their items do not fit in, they will have to take them out and repack them so that the lids close.

The train game

This is a fast and exciting game that can act as a prelude to a discussion on travel and other cultures.

Resources

Names written on card for the destinations from Holidays (see page 105) – Badgerwood, Clifftops, Lower Westway and Seaview.

What to do

Place the destination names at different points around the room. The children put their chairs in pairs in the centre of the room, one pair behind the other to represent the seats on a train. While you say the verse below, the children move their outside arms round in unison like the pistons on a train. Start the verse quite slowly, then pick up speed as you continue to mimic the train moving faster.

> *Rocking, rolling, on the track.*
> *Ever faster, ever faster.*
> *On and on and far away,*
> *Taking us on holiday.*

At the end of the verse you say 'This is the station announcer. The train is now standing at . . .' Call out one of the stations. All the children leave the train and race to that destination. The last two to reach it are out and stand at the side of the room, helping you to say the verse next time. The remainder get back on the train. The winner is the last person remaining on the train.

Comments

Discuss with the children the value of travel. Discuss how different cultures have different values and how the children should respect these whilst visiting particular places on holiday.

Holiday snaps

In this activity the children need to work together to make a successful production, pooling their ideas and resources.

Resources

None

What to do

The children are put into their original groups for the holiday activity (see page 105). Explain to them that you want them to create a scene that will show the others the sort of things they would be doing on their chosen holiday. This can either be done as a tableau or a mime or by using dialogue. When they have rehearsed their scenes, they come back to the circle and show them to the others.

Comments

If the activity is done as a series of mimes, the other children could guess what they are doing. This could lead to a discussion about the need for compromise when on holiday if different people want to do different things.

Getting dressed

This activity is a fun way of reinforcing skills that help the children towards independence.

Resources

The children's jumpers or shoes

What to do

Divide the class into three teams and ask each team to sit in a circle. Ask the children to put either their jumpers or their shoes (do not use both in the same game) in the centre of the circle. On your command, one child in each circle goes into the centre to retrieve and put on their item of clothing. When this has been achieved satisfactorily (shoes have to be fastened properly), the child returns to their place and the next child goes to the centre. The activity continues until one team has all its members fully clothed and seated. That team is the winner.

Comments

You can do this activity with several items of clothing so that, for example, all the children put on their jumpers, then begin again with their shoes.

Waiting

Children find waiting very tedious and quickly become bored and fidgety. This activity looks at ways of providing a different focus to waiting.

Resources

None

What to do

Do not tell the children that the object of the activity is to find ways of helping them to stand still and quiet. Ask them to line up and leave them until you sense they are beginning to get restless. Tell them to spread out. Allowing a few minutes for each, ask them to shut their eyes and think about the following suggestions:

> The most delicious meal they can imagine.
> Going over their times tables in their heads.
> Having fun on holiday.
> Planning what they will do when they get home that day.
> Counting sheep passing through a gate.
> Opening the best birthday present they can think of.

Call the children into a circle. Explain to them what you noticed when they lined up initially. Ask them which of the things they imagined they found the most absorbing. Do they think they could use strategies like these as distractions when waiting?

Comments

Suggest to the children different things to think about when there is a delay while they are waiting in line, so that it becomes common practice for them.

Positions, please

This is a entertaining way of practising standing still that you
could incorporate into your teaching.

Resources

None. Plenty of space to play in is needed.

What to do

Ask the children to spread out in the playing area. Tell them that
you will ask them to take up various positions, which they must do
without moving from the place they are standing in. Anyone who
does move from their standing position is out. You could use the
following suggestions:

> Skiing
> Riding in a horse race
> A ballet dance
> Diving into a swimming pool
> Throwing a ball
> Washing a car

Continue with the game until one child is left. They are the winner.

Comments

You could use this activity as a regular way of getting the children
to be still and quiet, using different examples each time to surprise
and amuse them. You could use it to break up an activity that
requires a lot of concentration, too.

I'm so cross

This activity is an enjoyable game and can provide lots of hilarious moments for the children.

Resources

None

What to do

The children sit in a circle. They volunteer amusing and far-fetched ways of completing the sentence stem 'I'm so cross I could . . .' Give them some examples such as:

roar louder than a lion
jump up and down as high as a mountain
scream loud enough for them to hear me in Australia
shout my socks off.

Tell the children that one of the best antidotes to anger is laughter. Perhaps when they feel angry, they could think of one of these examples instead.

Comments

You could use this game with the children as an introduction to anger management.

A state of independence

This activity focuses the children's attention on the process of growing up and becoming independent.

Resources

A flipchart and marker pen

What to do

Brainstorm with the children the skills they think they will need to be independent adults. These could include travelling on their own, managing money, managing a home, dressing themselves, taking care of personal hygiene, shopping, cooking. Ask them about how they learn these skills. Discuss why they learn things at school and what this equips them for. Ask the children to evaluate how far along the road to independence they think they are at present. Get them to decide what the most important skills they have learned are and which ones they still have to learn.

Comments

Ask the children what they think will be the rewarding and the difficult things about being an independent adult.

Reflections

This activity involves the children in a self-evaluation exercise, giving them the opportunity to consider areas in which they could improve.

Resources

A questionnaire and a pencil for each child in the group (see page 142)

What to do

Give each child a copy of the questionnaire to fill in. Tell them to be as honest as they can. When they have done this, ask them to come back to the circle, choose one area that they think they could improve on and discuss how they could achieve this. If they need help, they could ask for suggestions from others in the circle to help them move forward. Make a list of the group's resolutions for display and evaluate their progress in future at intervals.

Comments

If you are feeling brave, you could join in this activity and add a resolution of your own to the list.

Further activities

Animal skills

Put the children into pairs or small groups and ask them to investigate a bird or animal, discovering the skills that the young need to acquire to prepare them for adulthood.

When I'm grown up

Ask the children to imagine how they will be as adults. Ask them to think of what occupation they will have, what sort of house they would live in and what goals they need to set themselves to reach this position.

Sheep and lambs

The children stand in a large circle holding hands. Two children are chosen to be the sheep and wear blindfolds. Three other children are chosen to be lambs. The sheep and lambs are in the centre of the circle. Every time the sheep 'bleats', the lambs must answer. The object of the game is for the sheep to find a lamb. The other children hold hands to keep the players in the circle. When a sheep has found a lamb, the game begins again with new players.

I went on holiday and took . . .

Play a memory game around the circle. The children say 'I went on holiday and took . . .' Each child names all the items previously chosen and adds a new one to the list. When a child is unable to remember all the preceding items accurately, they begin a new list.

Snapshots

Let the children bring in holiday photos to show to each other. They could make a wall display of them.

Celebrating together

This final section is a celebration of coming together and enjoying one another's company. The activities focus on the good things that people participate in together, playing games purely for fun and to create a warm feeling within the group.

Let's pretend

This is a lively game that encourages group cooperation and creative thinking.

Resources

Several items such as a cardboard box, a plastic bottle, a plastic plate, a bag. You need enough to give one item to each group. Pencils and paper for each group.

What to do

Divide the class into mixed-ability groups of 5 or 6. Explain to the children that each group will have an item. They have to pretend that their item is as many different objects as they can think of – for example a box could be a television, a dog's bed or a planter. One child in each group notes down their group's ideas. Allow 5 minutes for this and give each group a different item. Continue like this until each group has covered all the items. Bring the children into a circle and ask them to volunteer their suggestions for each item.

Comments

It is important to have mixed-ability groups for this activity to help those children who might find it difficult to think of ideas.

Jumping Jacks

This game is fun, although it does require concentration and the children must stay alert.

Resources

None. Plenty of space to play in is needed.

What to do

One child is chosen to be the watcher and stands facing a wall. The other children are Jumping Jacks and line up against the opposite wall. While the watcher is turned away, the Jacks can move forward, but only by jumping. If the watcher turns round and sees any of them moving, they will be sent back to start again. The Jacks therefore have to be watchful and stop moving as soon as they see the watcher beginning to turn. The first Jack to reach the end and touch the watcher without being detected becomes the new watcher.

Comments

You could play the game with different movements, such as crawling cats, bunny-hopping rabbits, wiggling worms.

I'm so happy

This activity is intended to create a feel-good atmosphere within the group.

Resources

None

What to do

The children sit in a circle and volunteer amusing and far-fetched ways of completing the sentence stem 'I'm so happy I could . . .' Give them some examples such as:

laugh like a hyena
hug a giant
kiss a tarantula
dance to Timbuctoo and back again.

Comments

Ask the children to describe what it feels like to be happy and what makes them happy.

Three's a crowd

This is a fast, frantic game played just for fun.

Resources

None. You need plenty of space to run around in.

What to do

Divide the children into two equal teams. Make sure that if one child is left over, they are included the next time the game is played. Ask one team to stand in a large circle. Ask the second team to form an outer circle, each child standing behind a child in the first circle. Choose two children to start the action. One child chases the other in and out of the circle. When the child who is being chased becomes tired, they stand in front of any child in the inner circle. This creates a line of three children, so the child at the end – the one in the outer circle – must take up the action and become the chaser. The child who is chasing must always be alert and ready to change roles. If a chaser catches a child, start again with two new players.

Comments

If the circles start to creep in and become smaller, stop the action during a changeover and move the children out again.

Human animals

This activity focuses the children's attention on the positive qualities that people possess.

Resources

Paper and pencils

What to do

Divide the class into groups of 5 or 6, giving each group a piece of paper and a pencil. Tell the groups that they are aliens who have come to investigate all the animals that live on Earth. Ask the children to list all the positive qualities they think humans have that would make them seem superior to animals. Tell them to pay particular attention to social habits. Call the children back to the circle to discuss their findings.

Comments

You could ask the children if they think there are any qualities that some animals have that people would do well to copy.

Our great group

This activity is intended to create a warm feeling by celebrating each child's inclusion in the group.

Resources

None

What to do

The children stand in a large circle. One child takes a step forward, turns to the child on their left and encourages them to step forward also. The second child does so and holds the hand of the first child. This process is repeated around the circle until all the children are holding hands. On command the children raise their arms and say together:

> *Two, four, six, eight, we are here to celebrate.*
> *One, three, seven, nine,* [name of group] *is really fine.*

Comments

Talk to the children about bonding activities and ask them why they think they are important and beneficial for groups of people. Get them to think of examples, such as football chants, joining in songs at pop concerts.

The dice game

This active game is just for fun.

Resources

A large spotted 1–6 die

What to do

Choose one child to be in the centre of the circle. Number the remaining children 1 to 6 around the circle. The child in the centre rolls the die. All the children with the number shown on the die change places. The child in the centre tries to sit in an unoccupied place during the changeover and, if successful, takes on that number. The child left without a place goes into the centre to roll the die and the game continues.

Comments

You could use variations on this game to practise simple maths computations with younger children – such as number the children 1 to 5 around the circle, and use two dice and subtract the smaller from the larger number to arrive at the number that relates to the children.

On the ball

This is an activity for anticipation and enjoyment.

Resources

A softball, some music and a tape/CD player

What to do

The children sit in a circle. While the music plays, they pass the softball from child to child around the circle. The child who is holding the ball when the music stops must name a vegetable. Continue until the children have exhausted their knowledge of relevant names. You can do this with other categories such as animals and occupations.

Comments

A variation is to play the game alphabetically so that each vegetable named begins with the next letter of the alphabet. You could agree to leave out the very difficult letters before the game begins.

Celebrations

This activity looks at some of the different reasons why people come together to celebrate.

Resources

Books about festivals and celebrations. Examples are: *Starting with Me*, by Barbara Hume and Annie Sevier (Belair Publishing Ltd); *Festivals around the World*, by Godfrey Hall (Wayland Publishers); *Festivals*, by Jean Gilbert (Oxford University Press).

What to do

Look at some of the festivals and occasions that people celebrate – for example Christmas, Succoth, Diwali, Passover, Chinese New Year, Hogmanay, May Day, Harvest Festival, Mother's Day – and talk about what they do on these occasions, paying particular attention to the positive messages behind them. Divide the children into groups of 4 or 5 and ask them to think of a special school celebration. It could be the beginning or end of the school year or an invented occasion such as Achievement Day, Teacher's Day, School Community Day, Learning Day. Ask the children to think about when their celebration would be and what they would do. When the children have finished planning their occasion, call them into a circle and let each group talk about their celebration.

Comments

Choose one or more of the children's ideas as the basis of an actual celebration that they could organise and take part in.

New Year

This activity looks at the variation in one festival and shows the children how different races and cultures can celebrate the same occasion with many different customs. It begins with a focus on New Year, but other occasions would be suitable alternatives.

Resources

Pencil and paper for each group. A book about the festival, such as *New Year* by Jane Cooper (Wayland Publishers). This book looks at the different times and ways in which New Year has been celebrated by a variety of cultures around the world, both in the past and the present.

What to do

Look at and discuss the book with the children, paying particular attention to how varied the dates and customs may be for the same celebration. Put the children into groups of 4 or 5. Tell them that there is going to be a new celebration, World Day. The groups must think of why, when and how this will be celebrated. When the children have done this, call them into a circle and ask each group to explain or show what they have thought of.

Comments

Space the groups out and encourage them not to copy another group's ideas. Much of the fun of this activity is to see how varied the celebrations can be.

Let's party

This activity is an occasion when the class enjoys one another's company and celebrates being together.

Resources

Any items necessary for playing party games such as Musical Statues/Bumps, Dead Lions, Pass the Parcel, Squeak Piggy Squeak, Musical Chairs. Plastic cups and orange squash. Fortune cakes (buy or make small sponge cakes; into each insert a 'fortune' written on paper, such as 'You will have many good friends', 'You will have great happiness', 'You will enjoy many holidays', 'Your days will be filled with laughter').

What to do

Choose an occasion when the children have been working really well together to hold a party celebrating class unity. Play party games and have squash and cakes. Let the message of the party be that getting on with other people and doing things well together is the best way for people to live their lives.

Comments

Use this opportunity for children with less experience to practise social skills such as pouring drinks and handing out cakes.

Further activities

Games afternoon

Let the children use a selection of board and card games kept for special occasions. Encourage them to move around, trying different games with various partners.

Group motto

Ask the children to think up a suitable motto for their group. It must reflect the ideals they think they should be striving for. The motto could be written in large letters and displayed above the door.

Parachute games

Hold a parachute session as an opportunity for the children to work together. See *Making Waves* in the Training and resources section for further ideas.

Group magazine

Near the end of each term produce a group magazine that includes good pieces of work, other achievements, children's views and class news.

Photocopiable materials

Many of the resources are reused by the children. Ideally, they should be copied onto thin card.

Signal cards

List of mimes

Polishing my shoes.	Pegging out wet washing.
Sawing logs from a branch.	Making a cup of tea.
Writing on a flipchart.	Brushing a dog.
Putting food on a dish for a cat.	Hammering a nail into a piece of wood.
Making a sandwich.	Painting a portrait.
Mowing a lawn.	Building a sandcastle.
Phoning the police.	Changing a baby's nappy.
Buying something in a shop.	Mounting and riding a horse.
Digging up potatoes.	Eating an ice-cream.
Vacuuming the floor.	Comforting someone who is upset
Crossing a rope bridge.	Taking a dog for a walk.
Having a shower.	Skateboarding.
Climbing a mountain.	Making some toast in a toaster.
Hanging clothes in a wardrobe.	Going up in a lift.
Playing tennis.	Getting on a bus.

Shape cards

Story with cue words

Cue words

Benji: clap twice **Monkey**: tap knees three times
Palace: Stand up, sit down **Tail**: Stand up, turn around, sit down
Story: move two places to the right

India is a very beautiful country with many temples and **palaces**. This **story** takes place in a ruined **palace**. It was inhabited by a large and noisy troupe of **monkeys**. This particular group of **monkeys** was famous for their long, curly tails. The **monkeys** spent many hours grooming and admiring their splendid **tails** as they lay in the shade of the **palace** walls. The younger **monkeys** dreamed of the day when their **tails** would be as long and curly as their parents' **tails**. One of the young **monkeys** was called **Benji**. He liked to entertain the other youngsters by making up exciting stories. **Benji** was such a good **story** teller that **monkeys** from other troupes came to the **palace** to listen to his **stories**.

As the **monkeys** grew older their **tails** began to lengthen. All except **Benji**'s! His **tail** remained short and as straight as an arrow. The other **monkeys** soon noticed and started to whisper about it behind his back. Then, as time went on and **Benji**'s **tail** still would not grow and curl, they began to mock him openly. 'Look at **Benji**,' they cried. 'He has a **tail** like a dog's.' The other **monkeys** called him Woofy and laughed and pointed at him all the time. Poor **Benji**! Their cruel taunts made him sad. Finally, **Benji** could stand it no longer. One dark night, he slipped away from the ruined **palace** to find a hiding place where no one could make fun of him again.

At first the other **monkeys** did not really notice **Benji**'s disappearance, but as time went on they began to miss his wonderful **stories** and to ask each other where he could have gone. Of course none of the **monkeys** could answer this question. A wise old owl sat in the tree near the **palace** and knew everything that went on below. The owl told them that their unkindness about his **tail** had driven **Benji** away and he had gone into hiding. The **monkeys** felt very ashamed of their behaviour and set out at once to find **Benji**. When they found him they asked him to forgive them. After he heard how sorry the other **monkeys** were, **Benji** agreed to return to the **palace** and tell his wonderful **stories** again.

Fact cards

The Aboriginals live in Australia. They probably arrived there about 20,000 years ago. They lived like Stone Age people, hunting with spears. When the Europeans discovered Australia, most of the Aboriginal population died out.

Where do the Aboriginals live?
Did they arrive there 10,000,
20,000 or 30,000 years ago?
What did they hunt with?

Adders are poisonous snakes. They live in sandy places. They eat lizards, mice and voles. Males are yellow, brown or silvery in colour. Females are reddish brown to yellow. Young adders are born in September.

Where do adders live?
What colour are female adders?
When are the young born?

Ants are insects and have six legs. They usually live underground. They are very strong and can lift many times their own weight. They are very aggressive. Some species have raiding parties to attack other nests and some species take insect slaves.

Do ants have four, six or eight legs?
Where do they live?
Why do they have raiding parties?

Chameleons are lizards that live in trees. They catch insects with their long tongues. They can use their tails to grip branches. They can change the colour of their bodies to blend in with their surroundings. Their eyes can swivel in their sockets.

What do chameleons eat?
What is special about their eyes?
Where do they live?

Charles I became king of England in 1625. He reigned for twenty-four years. He fell out with Parliament. They fought each other. The king's supporters were known as Cavaliers and the parliamentary forces as Roundheads. Charles was beaten and later beheaded.

Charles I was king in 1800. True or false?
What were his supporters called?
How did he die?

Comets are made of ice and dust. There are millions of comets. They orbit the sun. The sun's heat makes comets turn into gas which forms a long tail. Halley's comet is the most famous, named in 1682.

What does the sun's heat do?
What are comets made of?
What is the most famous comet?

The cuckoo is a bird that lays its eggs in other birds' nests. The baby cuckoo hatches first and pushes the other eggs out of the nest. It increases its weight to fifty times its birth weight in three weeks. It flies to Africa for the winter.

Where does the cuckoo lay its eggs?
What does the baby cuckoo do to other eggs?
Where does the cuckoo fly for the winter?

The fire of London happened in 1666. It began in a baker's in Pudding Lane. More than a thousand buildings were destroyed by the fire in four days. The fire spread quickly because the houses were built close together and made of wood.

Did the fire start in 1066, 1666 or 1886?
How many houses were destroyed?
What were the houses built of?

Prompt cards

What is your favourite meal?	If you had £1000, how would you spend it?
Name a pop group that you like.	Talk about one of your hobbies.
What book do you really like?	What film have you enjoyed?
Where was your best holiday?	Which sport do you like playing most?
What do you like best in school?	What fruits do you like?
How would you describe yourself?	What is your favourite song?
Where would you like to visit?	What is one of your ambitions?
Whom would you most like to meet?	What would your ideal day be?
What is your favourite animal?	What clothes do you like to wear?
Which person from history do you most admire?	Name a film star you like.
Name a TV programme you like.	What is your favourite time of year?
What is your favourite drink?	What would you most like to buy?

Quiz

Questions	Points scored	
	Team 1	Team 2
What is 7 x 4?		
In which country is Paris?		
Who was Guy Fawkes?		
Is a crocodile a reptile or a mammal?		
Who is 007?		
What is a cuckoo?		
What is 19:00 hours on an analogue clock?		
Who is the President of the United States of America?		
What is Bart Simpson's mum called?		
What is the name of our queen?		
Who wrote the Harry Potter books?		
What would live in an eyrie?		
What do you play golf with?		
What are the young of a kangaroo called?		
Where is New York?		
Which is further north, London or Manchester?		
Who was Tarzan?		
What colours is a panda?		
What is 24 − 7?		
Cleopatra was queen of which country?		
What is Robbie Williams famous for?		
What is an oak?		
What is the biggest land animal?		
What is a diamond?		
How many blackbirds were baked in a pie?		
What is broccoli?		
Does a polar bear live somewhere hot or somewhere cold?		
Who wrote *The BFG*?		
How many tentacles does an octopus have?		
What did the farmer's wife do to the three blind mice?		
Who was Robin Hood?		
Is marmalade sweet or savoury?		
What do you use a parachute for?		
What is the name of the Prime Minister?		

Category cards

Pets	Pop stars or groups	Sports
Birds	Animals	Clothes
Weather	Books	Films
Vegetables	TV programmes	Countries
Film stars	Cartoons	Colours
Puddings	Family members	Sweets
Tools	Funfair rides	Transport
People from history	Sports	Trees
Occupations	Toys	Songs
Furniture	Buildings	Cars

Paired cards

Hot	Cold	Fat	Thin	Big	Little
Up	Down	Under	Over	In	Out
Wet	Dry	Happy	Sad	Good	Bad
Powerful	Weak	Ill	Well	Black	White
High	Low	Sunny	Rainy	On	Off
Rough	Smooth	Rich	Poor	Pretty	Ugly
Straight	Crooked	Fast	Slow	Tall	Short
Brave	Cowardly	Wise	Foolish	New	Old

Shapes page

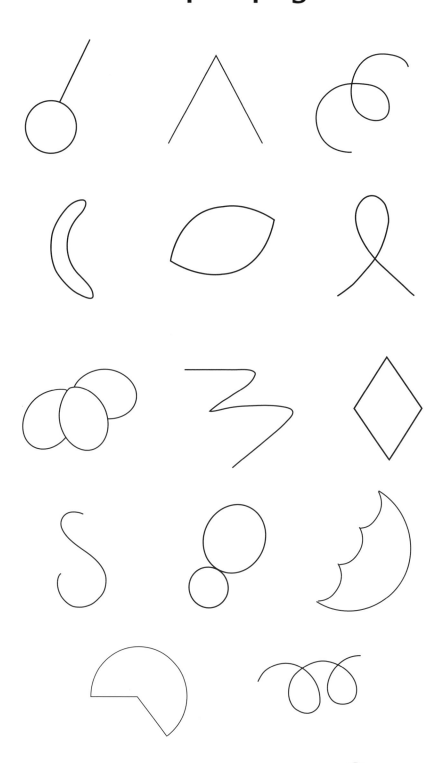

Shop cards

A newsagent You sell papers and magazines

A greengrocer's shop You sell fruit and vegetables

A chemist's shop You sell medicine and drugs

A baker's shop You sell bread and cakes

A toy shop You sell toys

A shoe shop You sell footwear

A card shop You sell cards and wrapping paper

A gift shop You sell fancy goods such as ornaments

A jeweller's shop You sell jewellery and watches

A fishmonger's shop You sell fresh fish and seafood

A bicycle shop You sell bicycles

A DIY shop You sell paint, wallpaper and tools

An art shop You sell paint sets, pencils, art kits, crayons and paper

A supermarket You sell food

A pet shop You sell pets and pet food

A book shop You sell books

A furniture shop You sell household furniture

Trios cards

You are a film star.	**You are an alien.**
You like acting.	You live on planet Eon.
People go to the cinema to see you.	You are not an earthling.
You are a dog.	**You are a juicy, red apple.**
You chase cats.	You grow on a tree.
You get taken for walks on a lead.	You are healthy to eat.
You are a book.	**You are a bed.**
People read you.	People lie down on you.
You are full of stories.	You are soft and comfortable.
You are a necklace.	**You are a sausage.**
You are worn around the neck.	You are cooked on a barbecue.
You are made of gold and jewels.	You are meaty.
You are a car.	**You are a pair of scissors.**
People ride in you.	You cut things.
You have four wheels and an engine.	You have fingerholes and two blades.
You are a pair of boots.	**You are a doughnut.**
You keep feet dry.	You are covered in sugar
People wear you in the rain.	You are made by a baker.

Questionnaire

Place an x along the continuum for each item.

	Poor	Average	Good

Asking adults for things. ....

Talking in front of others. ....

Joining in games. ....

Contributing to discussions. ....

Respecting other people's views. ....

Finding ways to amuse myself. ....

Listening well. ....

Making friends. ....

Sitting still. ....

Waiting my turn. ....

Trying new things. ....

Saying kind things to others. ....

Mixing with people I don't know. ....

Being able to concentrate. ....

Learning independence skills. ....

Showing sympathy for others. ....

Knowing when to keep quiet. ....

Being patient. ....

Having good manners. ....

Doing things for myself. ....

Bouncing back after setbacks. ....

Trying again and again. ....

Staying calm under pressure. ....

Looking on the bright side. ....

Having confidence. ....

Training and resources

Jenny Mosley INSET courses

The following courses and workshops are available from a team of highly qualified and experienced consultants, who can be contacted through:

Jenny Mosley Consultancies
28a Gloucester Road
Trowbridge
Wiltshire   Tel: 01225 767157
BA14 0AA   Fax: 01225 755631

Email: circletime@jennymosley.demon.co.uk
Web site: www.circle-time.co.uk

Promoting happier lunchtimes
Turn your school round – an introduction
A whole-school approach to building self-esteem through Circle Time
Assessing the effectiveness of your self-esteem, anti-bullying and
   positive behaviour policies
Raising staff morale through team-building
Practical activities to maintain and develop the power of Circle Time
A workshop of games to enrich class and lunchtimes.

Training support for your workplace

The Jenny Mosley Consultancies' well-trained personnel, experienced in all aspects of the Quality Circle Time Model, are available to visit your workplace to give courses and workshops to all your teaching and support staff. We run both closure and in-school days. In the closure day, all staff, teachers, teaching assistants, lunchtime supervisors and administrative staff are invited to explore how to develop team-building and moral values through Golden Rules, incentives and sanctions, and ideas for happier lunchtimes.

During the in-school day the school does not close and the Quality Circle Time method is demonstrated with whole classes of children, observed by a range of staff. In addition to this, Circle Time meetings are held for lunchtime supervisors and an action plan for the school is considered with key members of staff.

Training the trainer courses

Key people may be trained to go back either to their school or their LEA as accredited trainers, responsible for supporting all adults and children in their community through the Jenny Mosley model. For details of on-going courses contact Jenny Mosley Consultancies on 01225 767157.

Quality Circle Time training manuals and resources

Mosley, J. (1998) *More Quality Circle Time*, LDA
Mosley, J. (1998) *Quality Circle Time*, LDA
Mosley, J. (1993) *Turn Your School Round*, LDA
Mosley, J. and Sonnet, H. (2002) *101 Games for Self-Esteem*, LDA
Mosley, J. and Sonnet, H. (2002) *Making Waves*, LDA
Mosley, J. and Thorp, G. (2002) *All Year Round*, LDA
Mosley, J. and Thorp, G. (2002) *Playground Games*, LDA
Mosley, J. and Thorp, G. (2002) *Playground Notelets*, LDA
Goldthorpe, M. (1998) *Effective IEPs through Circle Time*, LDA
Goldthorpe, M. (1998) *Poems for Circle Time and Literacy Hour*, LDA
Goldthorpe, M. and Nutt, L. (2000) *Assemblies to Teach Golden Rules*, LDA

Mosley, J. (2000) *Quality Circle Time in Action*, LDA
Mosley, J. (2000) *Quality Circle Time Kit*, LDA
Mosley, J. (1996) *Class Reward Sheets*, LDA
Mosley, J. (1996) *Golden Rules Posters*, LDA
Mosley, J. (1996) *Responsibility Badges*, LDA
Mosley, J. (1996) *Reward Certificates*, LDA
Mosley, J. (1996) *Stickers*, LDA

For information about the full range of Jenny Mosley's books and resources, please ring LDA Customer Services on 01945 463441.